Victorian
and
Modern Poetics

Victorian
and
Modern Poetics

Carol T. Christ

THE UNIVERSITY OF CHICAGO PRESS
Chicago and London

The University of Chicago Press, Chicago 60637
The University of Chicago Press, Ltd., London

Library of Congress Cataloging in Publication Data

Christ, Carol T.
  Victorian and modern poetics.

  Includes index.
  1. American poetry—20th century—History and
criticism. 2. Eliot, T. S. (Thomas Stearns), 1888–1965—
Criticism and interpretation. 3. Pound, Ezra, 1885–1972
—Criticism and interpretation. 4. Yeats, W. B.
(William Butler), 1865–1939—Criticism and interpreta-
tion. 5. English poetry—19th century—History and
criticism. 6. Modernism (Literature) 7. Romanticism—
England. I. Title.
PS324.C47 1984   821'.912'09   83-18200
ISBN 0-226-10458-3 (cloth); 0-226-10459-1 (paper)

. . . the men or the times that serve life in this way, by judging and annihilating the past, are always dangerous to themselves and others. For as we are merely the resultant of previous generations, we are also the resultant of their errors, passions, and crimes: it is impossible to shake off this chain. Though we condemn the errors and think we have escaped them, we cannot escape the fact that we spring from them.

Nietzsche, *The Use and Abuse of History*

Contents

Acknowledgments

I would first like to thank the participants in the two summer seminars in Victorian and modern poetics that I taught for the National Endowment for the Humanities in 1980 and 1982. Their vigorous discussion of the problems that I was addressing did much to shape this book.

Michael Bernstein, Zelda Boyd, Josephine Miles, David Miller, Morton Paley, Larry Sklute, and Alex Zwerdling read this manuscript in various stages of completion. I am grateful for the many suggestions that they made to improve it.

Finally I would like to thank the National Endowment for the Humanities for a fellowship that enabled me to take the leave during which most of this book was written.

1

Introduction

To Ezra Pound the Victorian Age, like the rest of the nineteenth century, was "a rather blurry, messy sort of a period, a rather sentimentalistic, mannerish sort of a period."[1] T. S. Eliot, too, dismisses the Victorians. After describing the dissociation of sensibility which for him characterizes poetry since the seventeenth century, he credits Keats and Shelley with struggling toward unification. "But Keats and Shelley died, and Tennyson and Browning ruminated."[2] Yeats also criticizes the "psychology, science, moral fervour" of Victorian poetry.[3] The anti-Victorianism of the chief Modernist poets is well known, in large part because it was incorporated into the New Critical vision of poetic history. In the "Notes for a Revised History of English Poetry," which ends *Modern Poetry and the Tradition*, Cleanth Brooks uses the concept of dissociated sensibility to discredit the achievements of Romantic poetry. The Victorians provide him with the most extreme example of the poetic failures he describes.

> Victorian poetry hardly calls for extended comment here. The points to be made against it on the basis already set forth are perfectly obvious, and have been made often. . . . The motive here is not to add anything to the indictment, but merely to relate the poetry of the Victorians to the foregoing pattern.
>
> Victorian poetry does offer occasion for a convenient summary; for, if poetry since the Restoration has been characterized by a confusion between imaginative and scientific organization, the Victorian period will furnish an illustration of this confusion in its final and most extreme form. Poetry is left impaled on one of the two horns of the

1

dilemma: poetry with a message, the "philosophy" of Tennyson and Browning—the attempt to substitute poetry for
religion; or, on the other hand, pure poetry, art for art's
sake.[4]

Brooks was speaking in 1939. In 1965 he wrote "A Retrospective
Introduction" for a new printing of the book in which he comments on his earlier views. He asserts that were he rewriting the
book today, he would want to lay more stress "on the extent to
which Eliot, Yeats, and the other modern poets built upon the
Romantic tradition and incorporated structural devices that are
a part of the general Romantic inheritance."[5] He does not mention the Victorians in his retrospective revaluation.

Recent scholarship in literary history has largely followed the
pattern which Brooks's retrospection suggests. There has been
an elaborate and subtle revaluation of the complex relationship
between Romantic and modern poetry in the work of Frank
Kermode, Robert Langbaum, Harold Bloom, and George
Bornstein among others.[6] But the poetry of the Victorians has
been either neglected in these discussions, thereby giving covert
support to the Modernist view of the Victorian period, or assimilated to the Romantic tradition. Kermode treats Pater, Rossetti,
and even Arnold as transmitters of Romantic thought; in his
study of Yeats, Bloom uses the work of Pater and Rossetti to
explain the beginning of Yeats's transition from nineteenth- to
twentieth-century Romanticism. Langbaum is the one critic who
gives prominence to the Victorians in his treatment of the relationship of the nineteenth and twentieth centuries, but he too
assimilates Victorian poetry to a Romantic tradition in his argument that the poetry of the nineteenth and twentieth centuries
can be seen as a poetry of experience.

Victorian and Modernist poetics do indeed define themselves
within a Romantic tradition which modern criticism has admira-
bly described. But in emphasizing the Romantic premises at the
base of modern poetic thought, much literary history ignores
the specific character of the Victorian poetic heritage. The Victorians and the Modernists find the prominence which they feel
that Romanticism gives to the poet's subjectivity burdensome
and restrictive. Even while they write within a Romantic tradition, each of the major Victorian and Modernist poets reacts
against the subjectivity which he associates with Romanticism by

attempting to objectify the materials of poetry. Arnold constructs a theory of appropriate poetic subjects—great actions, independent of time—to safeguard poetry from the limitations imposed upon it by the mistaken attempt to write only "an allegory of the state of one's own mind."[7] Both Arnold and Tennyson use myth and legend to attain a resonance and objectivity greater than mere personal emotion could offer. Browning and Tennyson evolve forms of the dramatic monologue to separate the poet from the poem and thus objectify its presentation of personality. Likewise the chief Modernist poets seek an objective basis for poetry's presentation of emotion. Eliot evolves the theory of the objective correlative whereby the poet presents not his personality but his medium. Like the Victorians, he uses the dramatic monologue extensively, and he seeks first in myth, then in orthodox Christianity, an objective means of structuring and evaluating the particulars of history. Pound's personae build upon the discoveries of Browning's dramatic monologues. In his research into Chinese written characters, Pound seeks a natural language which represents subjective and objective with equal transparency. In his attempt to write a historical epic, Pound develops what he calls "the method of Luminous Detail," by which facts that carry their own significance reveal the meaning of history. Even Yeats, the most Romantic of the Modernists, uses the supernatural to validate mask and symbol. Like the Victorians, the Modernists modify their Romantic heritage by seeking a more objective basis for poetic discourse. In so doing they evolve poetic strategies that resemble those of the Victorians: constructs of mask and persona which, like the Victorian dramatic monologue, distance the poem from the poet; theories of image and symbol which identify sensuous perception with the qualities of objects themselves; theories of language which emphasize its transparency as a medium for sensation; structures of myth and history which provide a narrative that contains and gives significance to personalities. Despite their anti-Victorianism, Modernist poets explore ways of objectifying poetry that show striking continuities with Victorian poetics.

Before I explain how their departures from Romanticism lead the Victorians and the Modernists to similar poetic strategies, I will define the ways in which they both operate within a Romantic tradition. Romantic poetry takes its materials and its shape from imaginative experience. Whatever differences separate the

English Romantics, they share a belief in the imagination as the generative source of poetry's substance and form. The typical Romantic lyric—"Tintern Abbey," "Dejection: An Ode," "To a Sky-Lark," "Ode to a Nightingale"—enacts the poet's self-discovery at a moment of imaginative contemplation. The Victorians and the Modernists, as we shall see, react with varying degrees of discomfort to the Romantic conception of the imagination, but they are nonetheless concerned in their poetry with mental acts.[8] Browning's and Tennyson's dramatic monologues, Arnold's lyrics, Yeats's lyrics, Eliot's dramatic monologues, Pound's personae primarily concern what happens in their speakers' minds as they confront an event or experience and take their form from the play of that mind. However different they are in the relationship of speaker to poet and of mind to nature from Romantic poetry, they are nonetheless like poems of the Romantics which reenact imaginative experience.

In Romantic poetry the imagination most often comes to its discovery in contemplation of an image—a leach gatherer, the west wind, a Grecian urn, frost at midnight. Romantic poetry portrays its contemplation of the image as the mind's way of realizing its relationship to reality. In *Romantic Image* Frank Kermode locates the continuity between nineteenth- and twentieth-century poetry in a belief in the image as a radiant truth out of space and time. Indeed, as Kermode argues, a belief in the image as poetry's way of knowing is central to Pound's imagism, Eliot's objective correlative, and Yeats's concept of the symbol. Kermode treats Arnold, Rossetti, Pater, and Wilde as the important transmitters of the Romantic conception of the image in the Victorian period, but Tennyson and Browning are also concerned with the image in a way directly continuous with Romantic poetry. In his review of Tennyson's early poetry Arthur Henry Hallam defines Tennyson as a "picturesque" poet in the tradition of Shelley and Keats. Although no contemporary critical tradition associates Browning with the Romantic image, Browning's speakers frequently use images, as I shall argue, in ways that recall Romantic poetry.

The focus upon mental action and upon the image shows how central the relationship of subject and object is to Romantic poetry and thought. In the classic statement of Romantic poetics, M. H. Abrams argues that the Romantics understand the activity of the perceiving mind not as a mirror reflecting the external world but as a lamp projecting its light, creating as it sees, and thus unifying subject and object.[9] But, as much criticism subsequent to Abrams has shown, the imagination, seeking experience of the mind's union with nature, often realizes only a troubled consciousness of its own priority.[10] Even as they celebrate the spousal union of man and nature, the Romantics fear that the self may be forever alienated from the objects it perceives. The mind's realization of its own autonomy as it attempts to approach the objects of its consciousness brings the Romantics to both a tragic awareness of the solitary self and a compensatory exaltation in the imagination's power.

The Victorians could not feel this compensatory exaltation. The fear implicit in Romanticism that we may fail to know the objects of our consciousness, that we may realize only an eccentric and personal reality, motivates Victorian attempts to turn from what they perceive as a disabling focus upon the self. "Close thy *Byron;* open thy *Goethe,*" Carlyle's Teufelsdröckh urged;[11] Arnold would have repeated his advice. In the Preface to the 1853 edition of his poems, Arnold argues the inadequacy of the Romantic focus upon the self for what he understands as poetry's appropriate aim. The modern critic

> prescribes false aims. "A true allegory of the state of one's own mind in a representative history," the poet is told, "is perhaps the highest thing that one can attempt in the way of poetry." And accordingly he attempts it. An allegory of the state of one's own mind, the highest problem of an art which imitates actions! No assuredly, it is not, it never can be so: no great poetical work has ever been produced with such an aim.[12]

An allegory of the state of one's own mind too easily leads to "the dialogue of the mind with itself," in which "calm," "cheerfulness," and "disinterested objectivity" have disappeared.[13] The cure for this disabling inwardness, a fault that Arnold associates with his own *Empedocles on Etna,* lies in an art which imitates actions, "the external objects of poetry, among all nations and at all times."[14]

Of course, Arnold's conception of Romanticism, here and in other places, is a simplified one, distorted to fit his own purposes. Like a number of other Victorian writers, Arnold tends to associate Romanticism, when he is critical of it, with the disabling inwardness that he feared for himself. In order to motivate a personal change, he creates a historical plot, a movement from a misguided Romanticism, which has lost sight of art's highest values in its fixation upon the self, to a clarifying and regulating classicism. Browning's career reflects a similar pattern. He defines his chief Romantic influence, Shelley, as a "subjective poet" in a way that enables him to declare the time ripe for the emergence of the objective poet. Browning's opposition of subjectivity to objectivity results in a usefully simplified version of Shelley's enterprise, for, as in the case of Arnold, his simplification of Romanticism allows him to ground his own poetics on what seems to be a more secure foundation. However much Browning praises Shelley's "subjective" poetry, his own poetry reflects a fear of subjectivity's distorting power. *Pauline* ends in a manner that might illustrate Teufelsdröckh's cry:

> No more of the past! I'll look within no more—
> I have too trusted to my own wild wants—
> Too trusted to myself—to intuition.[15]

Browning's turn to the dramatic monologue seems to fulfill the intention that *Pauline* expresses, and the monologues themselves often associate the imagination's inner voice with madness. Tennyson also associates subjectivity with disabling inwardness.[16] Tennyson's speakers are often paralyzed within the illusions that their imaginations project, and Tennyson himself resorts to a number of poetic devices to set that inwardness in a controlling frame.

The Victorians' concern with what they feel are the dangers of Romantic subjectivity explains their various attempts to construct an epistemology which derives the feeling with which we respond to objects from the qualities of the objects themselves.[17] "To see the object as in itself it really is" is the business of the critical power, Arnold tells us.[18] He also reveres poetry for its power to show us nature, actions, events as they really are. We have already seen that Arnold criticizes the Romantics for too exclusive a preoccupation with the self. Even his praise of the Romantics shows an unwillingness to value subjectivity. Their best poetry, he argues, results from the transparency of their representations. In his essay on Wordsworth, Arnold writes:

Wordsworth's poetry, when he is at his best, is inevitable, as inevitable as Nature herself. It might seem that Nature not only gave him the matter for his poem, but wrote his poem for him. He has no style.[19]

And when Arnold praises Byron, he echoes his praise of Wordsworth:

When he warms to his work, when he is inspired, Nature herself seems to take the pen from him as she took it from Wordsworth, and to write for him as she wrote for Wordsworth, though in a different fashion, with her own penetrating simplicity.[20]

Arnold can talk of Romantic poetry as expressing nature rather than the poet by virtue of his conception of sincerity. He explains his praise of Wordsworth in the following way:

Nature herself seems, I say, to take the pen out of his hand, and to write for him with her own bare, sheer, penetrating power. This arises from two causes: from the profound sincereness with which Wordsworth feels his subject, and also from the profoundly sincere and natural character of his subject itself.[21]

A sincere poet like Wordsworth experiences things truly, that is, without the falsifying power of the insincere self. Arnold uses sincerity to naturalize the emotion that poetry represents. In doing so, he shows the discomfort he feels with the Romantic imagination. Arnold would like meaning to be a quality of the external world, not a creation of the informing mind. Other Victorian artists share Arnold's desire to verify feeling from the real qualities of objects. Ruskin's exhaustive inquiry into the truth of nature, his distrust of the overpowering emotion which leads weaker artists to indulge in the pathetic fallacy, the Pre-Raphaelite emphasis on the minutely accurate detail necessary to represent the truth of symbols, Tennyson's fidelity to nature all reflect a similar attempt somehow to anchor feeling in the qualities of objects rather than in the imagination of subjects. Much as the Victorians seek to transform the Romantic concern with self into an objective presentation of personality, they seek a theory of the image which identifies the feeling which an image produces with a quality of the outside world.

Modernist criticisms of the Romantics, like those of the Victorians, associate Romanticism with an eccentric subjectivity which cuts the artist off from both the real world and a communal tradition. In his essay in *The Sacred Wood* on the Romantic criticism of George Wyndham, T. S. Eliot writes:

> What is permanent and good in Romanticism is curiosity . . . a curiosity which recognizes that any life, if accurately and profoundly penetrated, is interesting and always strange. Romanticism is a short cut to the strangeness without the reality, and it leads its disciples only back upon themselves. George Wyndham had curiosity, but he employed it romantically, not to penetrate the real world, but to complete the varied features of the world he made for himself.[22]

Eliot argues that the emphasis which Romanticism places upon the individual imagination alienates the writer from tradition. The first paragraph of the "Introduction" to *The Sacred Wood* quotes Arnold's criticism of Romantic poetry from "The Functon of Criticism at the Present Time":

> It has long seemed to me that the burst of creative activity in our literature, through the first quarter of this century, had about it in fact something premature; and that from this cause its productions are doomed, most of them, in spite of the sanguine hopes which accompanied and do still accompany them, to prove hardly more lasting than the productions of far less splendid epochs. And this prematureness comes from its having proceeded without having its proper data, without sufficient material to work with. In other words, the English poetry of the first quarter of this century, with plenty of energy, plenty of creative force, did not know enough. This makes Byron so empty of matter, Shelley so incoherent, Wordsworth even, profound as he is, yet so wanting in completeness and variety.

Eliot continues in his own voice, "This judgment of the Romantic generation has not, so far as I know, ever been successfully controverted."[23] Eliot's essay on Blake, included in the same volume, makes a similar accusation.

Blake was endowed with a capacity for considerable under-standing of human nature, with a remarkable and original sense of language and the music of language, and a gift of hallucinated vision. Had these been controlled by a respect for impersonal reason, for common sense, for the objec-tivity of science, it would have been better for him. What his genius required, and what it sadly lacked, was a frame-work of accepted and traditional ideas which would have prevented him from indulging in a philosophy of his own.[24]

Eliot's attack on Romanticism springs from commitment to a classicism which he identifies with men's allegiance to "some-thing outside themselves," in government, in religion, and in lit-erature.[25] The relationship between Eliot's anti-Romanticism and his classicism is clear as early as his extension lecture series on modern French literature delivered in 1916. The outline of his first lecture argues that all the germs of Romanticism can be found in Rousseau. Rousseau's public career consisted of a struggle against "*authority* in matters of religion," and "*aristocracy* and *privilege* in government." His main tendencies were "exalta-tion of the *personal* and *individual* above the *typical*," "emphasis on *feeling* rather than *thought*," "humanitarianism: belief in the fundamental goodness of human nature," and "depreciation of *form* in art and glorification of *spontaneity*." His great faults were intense egotism and insincerity.[26] Eliot's association of insin-cerity with egotism recalls Arnold. The discomfort that both Eliot and Arnold feel with the imagination leads them to see personality as a potentially distorting medium, a temptation to a false self, which prevents the individual from seeing the object as in itself it really is, a phrase Eliot likes to quote from Arnold.[27] Unlike Arnold, Eliot associates the individual imagination with original sin. Listening to the inner voice that Romanticism re-veres leads to "doing as one likes," another phrase that Eliot quotes from Arnold, and "doing as one likes" leads to "vanity, fear, and lust."[28] Eliot characteristically uses Arnold to support a position more Hebraic and more anti-Romantic than Arnold's own. Nonetheless, their criticisms of the Romantics show a simi-lar pattern and serve a similar function. The idea which both poets construct of Romanticism enables them to shift the burden of personality to a discredited past while it allows them to claim a

9

more authoritative and objective foundation for their own poetics.

Pound's attitude toward Romanticism is harder to determine than Eliot's because he wrote so little about it. Where Eliot rewrites literary history by making an overt attack on the Romantics, Pound does so by omission.[29] The *ABC of Reading* lists only Crabbe and Landor as poets to be read between Pope and Browning. Pound devotes four pages to Crabbe, ten to Landor, and does not even mention any of the major Romantic poets. Nonetheless, Pound's attempt to create a countertradition to Romantic poetry through Crabbe and Landor suggests the values that he did not desire to locate in English Romanticism. He praises Landor for his classicism, for his conservation of tradition. And he praises Crabbe for his devotion to fact. He begins his essay on Crabbe by exempting him from a general condemnation of the literature of the last 150 years for its failure to value realism.

> "Since the death of Laurence Sterne of thereabouts, there has been neither in England nor America any sufficient sense of the value of realism in literature, of the value of writing words that conform precisely with fact, of free speech without evasions and circumlocutions."
> I had forgotten when I wrote this, the Rev. Crabbe, LL. B.[30]

Pound uses Wordsworth in the essay as a negative example against which he measures Crabbe. Wordsworth, Pound writes,

> was a silly old sheep with a genius, an unquestionable genius, for imagisme, for a presentation of natural detail, wildfowl bathing in a hole in the ice, etc., and this talent, or the fruits of this talent, he buried in a desert of bleatings.[31]

Presumably Wordsworth's contemplation of self and his philosophy of the imagination composed parts of that "desert of bleatings."

Yeats alone among the major Modernists sees himself in a Romantic tradition. Although his criticism of Victorian poetry resembles that of Pound and Eliot, he praises Romantic achievement and sets his own poetry in that context. But when he does criticize the Romantics, he criticizes them for a personal eccentricity in their philosophy and symbolism. He writes about Blake in a way that surprisingly anticipates Eliot, even in comparing Blake to Dante:

> He was a symbolist who had to invent his symbols; and his counties of England, with their correspondence to tribes of Israel, and his mountains and rivers, with their correspondence to parts of a man's body, are arbitrary as some of the symbolism in the *Axël* of the symbolist Villiers de l'Isle-Adam is arbitrary, while they mix incongruous things as *Axël* does not. He was a man crying out for a mythology, and trying to make one because he could not find one to hand. Had he been a Catholic of Dante's time he would have been well content with Mary and the angels.[32]

In a late essay on Shelley, he criticizes Shelley for not achieving an impersonal symbolic revelation, again contrasting his achievement to that of Dante.

> Shelley was not a mystic, his system of thought was constructed by his logical faculty to satisfy desire, not a symbolical revelation received after the suspension of all desire. He could neither say with Dante, "His will is our peace," nor with Finn in the Irish story, "The best music is what happens."[33]

Like the Victorians and like his fellow Modernists, Yeats wants to achieve an impersonal objectivity for his poetry and fears that Romanticism encourages a personal and eccentric use of images. He also criticizes a focus on personality that is not "more type than man, more passion than type.[34] It is to Yeats's credit as a reader of Romantic poetry that he does not associate a focus on the accidents of personality with any of the Romantic poets, but he is nonetheless concerned with transcending a merely egotistical poetry.

The criticisms that the major Victorians and Modernists make of Romanticism are central to an understanding of their poetic enterprise because they all write a poetry of mental action very much in the Romantic tradition. Their sense of the dangers of Romantic inwardness, of arbitrary and personal meanings, of alienation from tradition, motivates each of them to evolve strategies which establish a poetry of mental action in an objective context. The ways in which the Victorians and Modernists establish this context create important continuities between their poetics that have been obscured by the anti-Victorianism of Modernist poetics and much Modernist criticism. These responses stem from a similar conception, albeit an interestingly distorted one, of the dilemmas that they identify with Romanticism. Both generations of poets find the identification of the speaking voice of the poem with that of the poet a burden and a limitation. The Victorians evolve the dramatic monologue to separate the poet from the poem; the Modernists build upon Victorian achievements with the dramatic monologue in their construction of mask and persona. Much as the Victorians and the Modernists resist the limitation with which the poet's personal voice seemed to restrict the poem, they fear the dangers of a private and personal symbolism. Accordingly they strive to develop theories of the image in poetry which establish some objective ground for the feeling it generates. The actual operation of images in their poetry is far more ambiguous and complex than their theories suggest; Victorian and Modernist theories of the image attempt to rationalize an ambiguity in the way in which their poetry locates emotion. Finally, both Vitorians and Modernists seek in tradition some objective structure to contain their dramatization of psychological experience. They construct traditions out of very different materials—Tennyson from Arthurian legend, Browning from Renaissance history, Arnold from classical subjects, Yeats from Irish and Celtic materials, Eliot and Pound from an eclectic combination of mythology and history. Despite the diversity of sources and the individuality of the structures that they create, I shall argue that these traditions function in similar ways, particularly as they enable poets to shape long poems.

The three topics on which I have chosen to concentrate—dramatic monologue, mask, and persona; theories of image and symbol; constructs of myth and history—do not exhaust the similarities of Victorian and modern poetry.[35] I have chosen to concentrate on these three because they seem to me the most important ways in which the Victorians and the Modernists strive to establish a more objective context for poetic discourse than they felt was available to them in the Romantic tradition. In concentrating upon the continuities between Victorian and modern poetics, I have not attempted to describe the discontinuities between the two periods. The differences between Victorian and modern poetry in tone, in the use of irony, in decorum, in style, in density, to name just a few areas of contrast, are of course significant. But they have been so amply described that the break between the two periods has been exaggerated and the historical continuity obscured.

The fact of this exaggeration, the anti-Victorianism of Modernist poetics, will pose the final problem for my study. Given the continuities between Victorian and modern poetics, what then explains the Modernists' insistence on their radical break from Victorian poetry? My attempt to answer this question will bring me to the problem of periodization itself, the separation into historical epochs so characteristic of modern literature and criticism, for I am interested ultimately in understanding the constant historical comparison, the continual redefining of the modern, which characterizes modern literary history and in which we all participate. At the same time that I am constructing a literary history to illuminate the Victorian heritage of our own Modernism, I want to understand the nature of the formal, psychological, and historical imperatives that operate in the construction of literary history both for the poets with whom I am dealing and for us.

In my treatment of the Victorians, I have concentrated upon the work of Tennyson, Browning, and Arnold, for they compose the Victorian tradition as the Modernists understand it. In addition, I have used the work of Rossetti, Swinburne, and Pater, since their work also constitutes an important element of the immediate poetic past for the chief Modernists. I have been more selective in my treatment of modern poets, discussing only the work of Yeats, Pound, and Eliot because, more than other important Modernist poets, they define themselves within and against a British tradition. Each sees himself as rescuing poetry from Victorianism. It is significant that none of them is English, that Yeats wants to write a specifically Irish poetry, and that Eliot and Pound are Americans who seek to assimilate an international tradition. But in constructing his tradition, each sees himself as rebelling against the British Victorians and creating a new reading of English poetry. Yeats, as we shall see, has a different relationship to English literary history than either Eliot or Pound and repeatedly creates different resolutions to poetic problems. The contrast which he presents to Eliot and Pound is

important for my study because it suggests other ways of transforming the nineteenth-century tradition than Eliot and Pound
develop, while it makes the similarity in the directions he takes
all the more striking. Although the poetics of Wallace Stevens
and William Carlos Williams have important connections to the
various Modernist strategies that I describe, I have not treated
either poet. Because both of them identified themselves as
Americans, they did not undertake the battles against British
Victorianism in which Eliot and Pound engaged. Finally, I have
not chosen to treat the poetry of any number of minor figures
important in the history of the relationship and transition of
nineteenth- to twentieth-century poetry—Hardy, Housman, E.
A. Robinson, the poets of the nineties, to name just a few. This
study is not a history of the many complicated strands connecting the two centuries but is an argument about a way of constructing poetics that unites some of the major figures from
those centuries.

Most studies of Eliot, Pound, and Yeats have sought to understand their dependence upon the traditions they themselves
elect. I want to understand their dependence upon the Victorian
tradition against which they rebel. In so doing, I hope to show a
new way of reading Victorian and Modernist poetics which will
reveal the tensions and the choices they both share. If I have
constructed an argument that opposes Modernist constructions
of literary history, it is nonetheless an enterprise to which Modernist poetics commits us. In fulfillment of Arnold's request that
criticism continually create a climate for poetry, the criticism the
Modernist poets themselves write involves the reader in the reconstruction of the history its poetry uses as its materials. Eliot,
Pound, and Yeats each had the self-irony to realize that his poetry and criticism urged the reader to a reconstruction of even the
monumental position that it bestowed upon itself.

2

Dramatic Monologue, Mask, and Persona

In describing the development of modern poetry, Randall Jarrell writes that "the dramatic monologue, which once had depended for its effect upon being a departure from the norm of poetry, now became in one form or another the norm."[1] Yeats's conception of the mask, Pound's notion of persona, Eliot's extensive use of dramatic monologue all support Jarrell's assertion. Following in the tradition of Yeats, Pound, and Eliot, modern poets so characteristically separate the speaking voice of the poem from that of the poet that the concept of persona has become a central assumption of modern critical theory. Unlike most elements of Modernist poetics, the dramatic monologue has clearly acknowledged Victorian roots. Not only does critical discussion of the dramatic monologue argue a continuity between Victorian and modern uses of the form;[2] the principal Modernist poets themselves assert their continuity with a Victorian tradition. In his review of *Prufrock and Other Observations*, Ezra Pound praises Browning's *Men and Women* as "the most interesting poems in Victorian English" and goes on to contend that their form "was the most vital form of that period." He then puts Eliot's poetry in that tradition.[3] Conversely, Eliot asserts that Pound's experiments with persona derive from the influence of Browning.[4] Yeats speak of Wilde in connection with his idea of the mask,[5] and Wilde mentions the precedent of Browning.[6] It therefore seems appropriate to begin an investigation of the continuity of Victorian and modern poetics by exploring the relationship of the dramatic monoloue to Modernist constructs of mask and persona.

The origin of the dramatic monologue is a question of critical debate. Some writers treat it as a new form originating in the

Victorian period; others trace it to varied precedents, among them Ovid's *Heroides,* eighteenth- and nineteenth-century drama, the ancient rhetorical form of prosopopoeia, mono-drama.[7] As the debate about origins implies, writers also debate the exact definition of the form. In *The Poetry of Experience,* Robert Langbaum treats all modern poems which separate the speaker of the poem from the poet as dramatic monologues; A. Dwight Culler separates the dramatic monologue from mono-drama; Ralph Rader distinguishes the dramatic monologue from the dramatic lyric and from the mask lyric.[8] The diversity of evidence which has given rise to this critical debate suggests that many Victorian and modern poets, working from a variety of precedents and traditions, found it congenial to separate the speaker of the poem from the poet in a number of different ways. I am less interested in categorizing these modes of separa-tion than in asking whether they serve some common purpose which illuminates the relationship of Victorian and modern poetics.

In *The Poetry of Experience,* Robert Langbaum has given one important and suggestive answer to this question. The dramatic monologue, he argues, originates when the Victorian poet writes a Romantic lyric of experience in the voice of a character sepa-rate from his own. Like the Romantic lyric, the dramatic mono-logue contains a disequilibrium between experience and idea. The form forces upon us a conflict between sympathy and judg-ment. The conflict embodies the nineteenth-century poet's con-viction that imaginative apprehension gained through immediate experience is primary and certain, whereas the ana-lytic reflection that follows is secondary and problematical. The way in which the dramatic monologue emphasizes the primacy of experience explains why twentieth- century poets also find the form so congenial and continue its development.

Although Langbaum's placement of the dramatic monologue within the Romantic tradition makes clear the value which Ro-mantics, Victorians, and moderns all place on the primacy of individual experience, his argument leads him to minimize dif-ferences between the Romantic lyric and the dramatic mono-logue, differences which indicate a discomfort with the Romantic tradition that Victorian and modern poets share. Langbaum's identification of the Romantic lyric with the dramatic monologue depends upon our substituting the human character who speaks the monologue for the natural object that is the focus of the Romantic poet's meditations. In Langbaum's theory of the form, Browning's duke occupies the place of Wordsworth's landscape above Tintern Abbey or Shelley's Mont Blanc, offering a similarly authentic occasion for experience and problematic circumstance for reflection. But the fact that the poet does not present himself as a guide to experience or judgment in a dramatic monologue creates a crucial difference. Whatever problems of experience and subsequent reflection that Romantic poems concern, the poet nonetheless invites us to share those problems, offering himself as a significant guide to them. The poet of the dramatic monologue, on the other hand, withdraws from the poem, not offering himself as a source of value or judgment. Although the form may emphasize the experience of the speaker and perhaps even of the reader, it seeks to avoid the experience of the poet, the very subject which generates the Romantic lyric. We are indeed conscious of the poet's manipulation of his materials; we admire the skill of his craftsmanship or the brilliance of his performance, but we know nothing of his experience.

The way in which the dramatic monologue emphasizes the experience of the speaker, not the poet, implies two conflicting attitudes toward the status the poem claims for itself. On the one hand, the fact that the speaker presents an eccentric and personal vision of the world whose meaning cannot be fixed suggests an experiential and subjective sense of truth like the one Langbaum describes. On the other hand, the poet's dramatic presentation of material suggests an attempt to present it as an event not dependent on the personality of the poet or generated by his experience. The form at once emphasizes the subjective, historical, and relative nature of truth while it strives to escape that relativity and historicity by separating the poem from the experience of the poet. The dramatic monologue thus contains a far greater tension in its attitude toward personal utterance than that of the Romantic lyric. It at once emphasizes the relativity and contingency of truth while it strives to transcend that relativity by making the poem an object independent of the personality of the poet. It is this tension between a conviction that the poem is inevitably a personal utterance and a desire to give it the status of an object which unites the Victorians with the moderns in their evolution of poetic forms that separate the speaker of the poem from its writer.

Because the career of Robert Browning offers the clearest example of a self-conscious break from the form of Romantic poetry and because both poets and readers have so frequently taken his dramatic monologues as the model for the form, he is the poet with whom I will begin. Browning's first published poem, *Pauline*, is written in the Romantic confessional mode and is closely modeled on Shelley's *Alastor*. According to the familiar story, Mill's criticism of "the intense and morbid self-consciousness" of the poet[9] stung Browning into abandoning the self-revelation of Romantic spiritual autobiography for the more defended dramatic monologue, but the poem contains internal evidence as well which suggests why Browning ultimately turned from the form. *Pauline* concerns the joys and burdens which self-consciousness offers the aspiring poet. The speaker tells us that his soul is composed "of a most clear idea of consciousness / Of self" (269–70), which he experiences on the one hand as a "self-supremacy, / Existing as a centre to all things" (273–74) and on the other hand as a "principle of restlessness / Which would be all, have, see, know, taste, feel, all" (277–78).[10] In Keats's terms, the speaker feels conflicting urges toward the egotistical sublime and toward negative capability. Both urges meet inevitable frustration: "I cannot be immortal nor taste all" (810; 1833 text). Whether desiring to be God or experiencing the life of all his creatures, he confronts the frustration of his own finitude. The desire to encompass all the world results finally in the realization that one knows only the world the self encompasses. All of these paradoxes are familiar dilemmas of Romantic poetry. But in *Pauline* the guilt which the autonomy of self-consciousness imposes upon the speaker is extraordinary even for a poem in this genre. The speaker's desire for primacy and preeminence, what he calls his complete "commanding, for commanding" (817), repeatedly fills him with self-revulsion at the same time that he is unable to dispossess himself of it. This simultaneous preoccupation with self-worship and self-disgust provoked Mill's criticism of the poem. Browning's immediate and intense response to that criticism suggests that it struck some answering ambivalence in Browning himself toward the privileged egoism the poem represents, an ambivalence the poem reflects.

Browning responded to the conflict with which this egoism presented him by rejecting what seemed to him the subjective mode of Romantic confessional poetry for the more objective mode of the dramatic monologue. Whenever Browning described the dramatic nature of his poetry, he emphasized that his poems did not concern himself. He repeated the formulation that his poems were "dramatic in principle, and so many utterances of so many imaginary persons, not mine."[11] By detaching these "utterances" from his own person, he avoids presenting problems of self-consciousness in his own voice, but he remains preoccupied with such problems in the voices he creates. Browning portrays character after character engaged in the Romantic project of at once asserting the center of the universe that is "I" while being, having, seeing, knowing, tasting, feeling all. But these characters are typically so grotesque and eccentric that the poems emphasize not the discoveries but the limitations that self-consciousness involves. Browning's dramatic monologues characteristically concern the prison of self which the speaker constructs in attempting to encompass and control his world. "My Last Duchess," "The Bishop Orders His Tomb at St. Praxed's Church," "Andrea del Sarto," "Fra Lippo Lippi," "Childe Roland to the Dark Tower Came," "Caliban Upon Setebos," "Bishop Blougram's Apology" all reveal the inescapable self that encloses the speaker whenever and wherever he defines his universe in a way that reflects ironically upon the Romantic tradition of self-consciousness. For Browning, the dramatic monologue both expresses and distances the ambivalences self-consciousness evoked in him.

Browning's first dramatic monologues, "Johannes Agricola in Meditation" and "Porphyria's Lover," published in 1836, show the transformations he made in the Romantic confessional mode. Both poems are confessions in which the speaker attempts to justify himself. Johannes Agricola explains the special favor that God has bestowed upon him; Porphyria's lover explains his murder of Porphyria. Yet both poems recall specific passages from *Pauline*. "Johannes Agricola in Meditation" develops the feeling of God's special trust and love that the speaker of *Pauline* also voices. "Porphyria's Lover" recalls the assertion that Pauline's lover makes that he "might kill her and be loved the more" (902). Each of these passages in *Pauline* indicates the special privileges that the speaker feels belong to him by right of his poetic election. In the two dramatic monologues, to which Browning appended the title "Madhouse Cells" in 1842, he transforms that sense of special election to the pathology of insanity. Johannes Agricola and Porphyria's lover both take upon themselves the Romantic artist's prerogative to realize the world he imagines. The assurance which each of them feels that a special privilege justifies his creation only indicates how mad he is. Browning thus transposes the Romantic confessional poem into an ironic mode concerned with the solipsism implicit in the self's imaginings.

Like "Johannes Agricola in Meditation" and "Porphyria's Lover," many of Browning's subsequent dramatic monologues concern the self's attempt to possess and control the world. Frequently, a threat to the self's primacy or predominance occasions the monologue. In facing the possible affront a second wife might afford his pride, the duke of "My Last Duchess" explains how he dealt with his first wife's smiles. Andrea del Sarto tries to stay the cousin's whistle; Fra Lippo Lippi, the policeman's arrest. Bishop Blougram faces the challenge of Gigadibs; Mr. Sludge, that of his disillusioned client. The bishop of St. Praxed's Church confronts the ultimate limit of death and the control he will lose over his "nephews." In each monologue, the speaker uses the power of articulation to create a world that literally possesses and transforms whatever threatens the self's preeminence. But the transformation of speech does not always offer sufficient stability and control. In fact, the poems in which the speaker has only the resources of verbal apology, like "Bishop Blougram's Apology" or "Mr. Sludge the Medium," seem to extend themselves further and further, as if the project could have no end. Because the speaker gives up the attempt to manipulate a world in his own image when he stops talking, his stopping occasions anxiety. The poems divert themselves from their ends so that the speaker can sustain the tenuous power that speech affords.

As if to counter the fluidity and temporality of language, which undermines the stability of the self even while it asserts it, the speaker of the dramatic monologue often seeks to give whatever specific threat he encounters the stability of artistic reification. The duke makes his last duchess the portrait in his gallery. The bishop of St. Praxed's Church counters his fear of personal dissolution by transforming himself into his own tomb. Fra Lippo Lippi paints his world and portrays himself as the sly maker in the corner. But for all that, they fail. The duke tells us enough about his last duchess to create an image of her that escapes the control which he attempts to achieve in the portrait and that condemns him. After the bishop dies, he will have no control over the construction of his tomb. Fra Lippo Lippi evades failure only by a commitment to a vitality in life that exceeds the formulations of even his art. All three poems achieve whatever stability they possess not from the artifact that the speaker constructs but from the circling repetition that defines the self trying to fix its universe. Robert Langbaum has observed that dramatic monologues have no necessary beginnings and endings, but arbitrary limits.[12] As Langbaum implies, the poems rarely progress; the speaker seldom reaches a realization by the end of the poem unavailable to him at the beginning. Rather, the form has a circling quality that reveals by its repetitions the fixed elements of the speaker's identity. In "The Bishop Orders His Tomb," for example, the bishop's repeated assertions of pride at Gandolf's envy of his mistress, his sensual delectation of the materials of the church, the formula of resigned doubt, "Ah God, I know not," with which he faces evidence of his own guilt define and limit his character. He finally achieves not the stability and permanence that he hopes his death monument will grant him but the fixity of character that has been his from the beginning.

Browning thus uses the dramatic monologue to portray the ways in which the self circumscribes its world. In contrast to the Romantic lyric, in which the speaker witnesses the imagination's power by achieving a realization, an empathy, not his at the beginning of the poem, Browning's dramatic monologues confirm the imagination's reflexivity by converting everything to the formula it originally revealed itself to be. Often the very project that the speaker of a Browning monologue envisions parodies the Romantic quest. The speaker of "Childe Roland to the Dark Tower Came" discovers a landscape which he can only interpret through his paranoia. Caliban describing Setebos reveals the stunting anthropomorphism in any natural theology. Seeking the proof that the imagination offers of the self's extension and power, the speaker reveals the self's imprisonment. Seeking a transcendence beyond the self, the speaker achieves only the fixity of obsession. Even this fixity sometimes fails the speaker in his quest for permanence. The richest of Browning's dramatic monologues contain moments when even the self's formulations fail it, when language dissolves under the threat of the dissolution of identity itself. "The Bishop Orders His Tomb," for example, contains two moments when the bishop imagines not the tomb of his design but a tomb of "moldly travertine" smothering him like death itself. At the second of these moments, near the end of the poem, the formulas of the bishop's language fail him as he imagines his corpse in the tomb.

> There, leave me, there!
> For ye have stabbed me with ingratitude
> To death—ye wish it—God, ye wish it! Stone—
> Gritstone, a-crumble! Clammy squares which sweat
> As if the corpse they keep were oozing through.

The way in which syntax breaks down at this point shows that it participates in the very world of process that the speaker is attempting to resist. Like the speakers of many of Browning's monologues, the bishop relies upon language to objectify and monumentalize the self, but the connection of language to a world of subjective and temporal process makes it resist the speaker's designs. Not only does he fail to achieve the transcendence he imagines that his monument will give him; in his attempt to marmorealize himself, he reveals how difficult it is to sustain even the fixity of his egoism.

By the irony that Browning directs at his speaker's projects, he throws into question many of the claims the Romantic poet makes for the imagination. Browning's characters indeed construct worlds with the shaping spirit of their imaginations, but worlds so eccentric, so grotesque, that the poems emphasize not the truth but the delusion which springs from a privileged egoism. Even in poems like "Two in the Campagna," "Abt Vogler," or "A Toccata of Galuppi's," which do not direct extensive irony at their speakers in the manner of Browning's more flamboyant monologues, the separation of the speaker from the poet and the dramatic presentation of the occasion for utterance makes any lyrical statement which the poem contains relative to its particular circumstance. Browning thus stresses the historical moment, the contextual relativity, the evanescent quality of any lyrical utterance. His entire poetic enterprise in this way questions the nature and truth value of man's speaking for himself. Donning mask after mask, Browning explores the extension and limits of egoism.

Such a poetic enterprise involves the poet in a paradoxical situation because it implies that he can free himself of the constraints of his own personality to explore those of others. In his essay on Shelley, Browning asserts that this very separation between the man and his work characterizes the objective poet. Unlike the subjective poet, who produces a poetry "the very radiance and aroma of his personality, projected from it but not separated," the objective poet creates a poetry which "will of necessity be substantive, projected from himself and distinct."[13] In contrast to Shelley, the model for the subjective poet, Browning sees his own work as objective. In so classifying himself, he indicates how he would like to see his relationship to Romanticism. Although his poems concern, as I have been arguing, the dilemma of Romantic egoism, the form of the dramatic monologue, like the fiction of the objective poet, allows him to assume that his representation of those dilemmas will be objective, "projected from himself and distinct." The dramatic monologue simultaneously expresses tensions central to Browning's understanding of poetry and suppresses awareness of how problematic those tensions are by containing them within certain boundaries. By separating conflicts from his own personality and projecting them onto characters not only distinct but grotesquely dissimilar from himself, he distances and controls them. The form of his poetry at one and the same time expresses and evades the problem of Romantic subjectivity. In thus seeking the objectivity the form offers, Browning paradoxically shares the quest of many of his characters. Much as they frequently seek an objective correlative to the designs of the ego—a tomb, a portrait—so Browning seeks to objectify those designs in the portrait gallery he creates.

Although Browning may not intend the irony which he directs at his characters' projects to apply to his own, his poems nonetheless frequently express anxiety about the capacity of art and even language to embody truth. Mr. Sludge the Medium justifies his fakery by comparing himself not only to the poet who invents his world but to the prose writer, the dealer in common sense. Even they, Sludge asserts, cannot see the truth except through the distorting perspective of their egoism.

> Each states the law and fact and face o' the thing
> Just as he d have them, finds what he thinks fit,
> Is blind to what missuits him, just records
> What makes his case out, quite ignores the rest.

One might argue that Sludge has an interest in seeing the world in this way, that the distorting lens of his egoism represents truth as lie. But even the pope from *The Ring and the Book,* the most honest and scrupulous of Browning's characters, reflects that man's fallen condition contaminates speech. It is "barren words / Which, more than any deed, characterize / Man as made subject to a curse." Speech "still bursts o'er some lie which lurks inside" (348–51). Even in a hypothetical paradise, in which man has no societal inducement to lie, words cannot mirror things.

> But when man walks the garden of this world
> For his own solace, and, unchecked by law,
> Speaks or keeps silence as himself sees fit,
> Without the least incumbency to lie,
> —Why, can he tell you what a rose is like,
> Or how the birds fly, and not slip to false
> Though truth serve better? Man must tell his mate
> Of you, me and himself, knowing he lies,
> Knowing his fellow knows the same, —will think
> "He lies, it is the method of a man!"
> And yet will speak for answer "It is truth"
> To him who shall rejoin "Again a lie!"
> Therefore this filthy rags of speech, this coil
> Of statement, comment, query and response,
> Tatters all too contaminate for use,
> Have no renewing.
>
> (360–75)

Browning solves the dilemma of speech's lie by a spiritual vitalism which erupts through language though it is separate from it. Even Mr. Sludge admits a something that's truth, tricks and all. By intuition, the pope can weigh the seed of motive inspiring a deed and pierce through the lies and obscurities of the words that tell us the story. Characters in Browning's world, by commitment to the vital process of experience through which divine truth can manifest itself, can resist the delusion that personality, art, and language all foster. But personality, art, and language themselves compose necessary and inevitable form. Browning's poetry contains a tension between the embodiments inseparable from personality's articulation and the urge toward a vitalism that resists any single articulation.[14] Characters who admit this tension—the Englishman in Italy, Fra Lippo Lippi—achieve the greatest value Browning's world admits, and they provide a mirror of Browning's own enterprise. For Browning the constant process of assuming masks resists the rigidity and delusion that any one mask involves.

The form of the dramatic monologue thus allows Browning to mediate and control a number of related tensions. Because the dramatic monologue portrays an individual speaking at the same time that it composes a dramatic event, it can mediate between the subjective and the objective. On the one hand, the dramatic monologue reflects a newly problematic conviction of the subjective nature of perception which is the legacy of Romanticism. Through the delusions which the speakers betray, the form expresses a skepticism about the individual's ability to realize universal truth, a belief in the necessarily historical nature of utterance, a fear of the solipsism implicit in the mind's imaginings. On the other hand, the dramatic monologue provides the poet a way of achieving an objectivity and a range of experience that the voice of the poet no longer seems to offer. Browning uses the dramatic monologue to express and transform his Romantic heritage.

The potential that the dramatic monologue holds for at once admitting the subjective nature of perception while permitting the poet an objectivity and scope his own speaking voice no longer afforded him links Browning's use of the form to Modernist constructions of mask and persona. Through his development of a dramatic speaker distinct from the poet, Browning makes the poem less a statement by the poet than a particular event. Modernist poets, eager to avoid abstraction, to give the poem the status of an object rather than a statement, seize upon the potential in Browning's method as the center of their poetics. Before I move to early modern poetry, however, it remains to show that other Victorian experiments with voice resemble Browning's in the concerns that they express.

Tennyson is the other Victorian poet usually credited with the development of the dramatic monologue, despite the fact that he uses the form very differently from Browning. His career, unlike Browning's, does not show an abrupt shift to the dramatic monologue. From his earliest poems—"Memory," "The Exile's Harp," "Remorse," "Antony to Cleopatra," "Written by an Exile of Bassorah while sailing down the Euphrates"—Tennyson seems to have enjoyed assuming masks. A. Dwight Culler has shown that Tennyson's early experiments with speakers other than the poet derive from the ancient rhetorical form of prosopopoeia, in which the writer imagines what a particular historical or literary character might have said on a specific occasion and presents that character as actually speaking. Tennyson's mature dramatic monologues, which according to Culler should not be called dramatic monologues at all, combine the tradition of prosopopoeia with the contemporary rhetorical form of monodrama, a dramatic poem placed in the mouth of a single speaker, the aim of which is to display a range and variety of passions by using remarkable linguistic resources. Tennyson's poems, unlike Browning's, Culler argues, do not attempt to show individuality of character but phases of passion. They intend no irony; they evoke only wonder at the power of the passion and the skill with which the poet has realized its display.[15]

Culler's differentiation between the formal derivation of Tennyson's and Browning's use of speakers other than the poet makes clear many of the differences in their development of the dramatic monologue. (I use the single term for convenience.) Tennyson tends to draw his speakers from the world of myth rather than history. His poems tend to be more lyrical than dramatic. He uses whatever dramatic situation the poem contains not as an opportunity for revealing eccentricity of character as Browning does but as the occasion, in T. S. Eliot's words, for "stating an elegiac mood."[16] Tennyson's poems do not contain the elaborate irony of Browning's dramatic monologues, emphasizing the distance between the speaker's actual words and our understanding of those words. But they do achieve irony of another sort. Tennyson uses either narrative or legend to associate his speakers with madness or delusion. The story of *Maud*, the place of the Lotos-Eaters in the *Odyssey*, the portrait of Ulysses in the *Inferno*, the history of Fatima all identify their characters with some derangement. Tennyson thus dissociates himself from the emotion he depicts and makes it appear dangerous, excessive, forbidden.

By this dissociation, Tennyson, like Browning, uses the dramatic monologue to control and objectify the potential solipsism of personal vision. The speakers of Tennyson's monologues—Ulysses, Tithonus, the Lotos-Eaters, St. Simeon Stylites, the hero of *Maud*—are all cut off from their kind by absorption in some extraordinary emotion. Like Browning's characters, Tennyson's confront some threat to the way in which the self possess its world, although they experience the situation differently. Browning's characters engage themselves in a mad projection of the will to manipulate the world. Tennyson's characters typically fear that any attempt to engage the world will meet with blank unrecognition, absolute otherness. If the speakers of Browning's monologues seem mad with the possibility of infinite self-extension, Tennyson's speakers often voice a despair that there can be any meaningful interchange between the world and the self. Tithonus laments that he is cut off not only from his kind but from a world eternally young. The Mariners in "The Lotos-Eaters" fear that "our household hearths are cold." Ulysses ends the first verse paragraph of his monologue with the complaint that his people "hoard, and sleep, and feed, and know not me." The speaker of *Maud* despairs at his alienation from a "world in which I have hardly mixed." Each of these characters yearns for death to end the pain of his alienation, but he fears the annihilation of death much as he fears the world's failure to recognize him. The speakers of Tennyson's dramatic monologues characteristically poise themselves between the threat and the attraction that the world and death alike compose. The monologue becomes a way for the character to insulate himself from both fears by constructing a world of his own imagining which completely contains the self. It at once offers a narcissistic substitute for the world that is desired while it rationalizes rejection of that world. It protects the speaker from the pain of involvement in the very way that makes death attractive while it staves off death by the process of speaking.

It is easy to see how these paradoxes work in poems like "Tithonus" and "The Lotos-Eaters," which explicitly concern the speaker's difference from the world he inhabits and his yearning for oblivion. "Ulysses" no less concerns the self's desire to contain a world that carries the danger of both alienation and death. Ulysses turns from Ithaca because of the unrecognition that characteristically affects Tennyson's seers. He wants to construct a world that constantly declaims him: "I am become a name." "I am a part of all that I have met." Yet the untraveled world, the world that the self has not made its own, creates a constant anxiety prodding him forth on a voyage that can only end in death. Ulysses resists the limits that both the world and death impose by an eternal process of self-engorgement. Because any punctuation point implies a limit, the poem can barely afford the separation between present and future implied in the future tense. Therefore this poem about futurity stubbornly maintains itself in an eternal present. Like "The Lotos-Eaters," like "Tithonus," "Ulysses" suggests Tennyson's concern with the way in which man resists the world's difference from the self by reconstructing the world in his own image.

This concern makes clear Tennyson's kinship with the Romantics. Like Browning, he uses the dramatic monologue to explore the possibilities of solipsism which the Romantic imagination involves. The form offers him similar resources. By providing a means of objectifying self-absorption, it allows him to distance and control the dangers implicit for him in a poetry conceived as an allegory of the state of the poet's mind. Tennyson's poetry contains numerous morbid, self-enclosed characters like Mariana, the hero of *Maud,* and Fatima, who inhabit a landscape of their own imagining. The recurrence of such characters suggests an obsessive concern that the external world may exist only as the reflex of our consciousness. Tennyson defends against this possibility in his use of the dramatic monologue. By assigning the dilemma to a character objectively distinct from himself, he can objectify and control the burden of self-imprisonment that self-consciousness seems to impose.[17] The dramatic monologue further affords him a range of resonance which he can attach to the personal emotions that are his recurring concern. Tennyson gives the self-absorbing loss and the life weariness that engaged his imagination a universality by associating them with Ulysses, Tithonus, Mariana, Oenone.

The dramatic monologue remains a popular form throughout the Victorian period; many poets imitate and develop the model which Tennyson's and Browning's dramatic monologues suggest.[18] In the work of the Pre-Raphaelites, however, most notably in the poetry of Morris and Swinburne, the relationship of the speaker to the poet shows a significant change. Both Morris and Swinburne depend far less heavily upon irony to separate themselves from the speakers of their poems. Although Morris develops his use of the dramatic monologue from Browning's dramatic lyrics and romances, he changes the relationship of the lyrical utterance to the world of history which surrounds it. Whereas Browning's poems always play the speaker off against a historical context the knowledge of which he assumes he shares with the reader, Morris's speakers occupy a wasteland of disorder and violence which the reader understands little more than they do. I will take "Riding Together" as an example. In the poem, a Christian warrior narrates the story of a pagan attack upon his band, his companion's slaying, and his own imprisonment. Even in constructing so elemental a plot summary as this, however, I am falsifying the poem because the terms which it supplies are so minimal in defining any external context. It relates its action only in terms of the experiential process in which the speaker participates—"riding," "Together," "fought," "weather." We don't know where he is, who he is, what expedition he's involved in, who the pagans are, what prison ends his life. Unlike Browning, who portrays the experiential dimension of known historical figures and moments, Morris places experience in an unknowable history. Morris thus uses the dramatic monologue to reduce what is knowable to an intense intuition of scraps of experience whose historical totality no one understands.

As Morris develops the dramatic monologue from Browning, so Swinburne develops it from Tennyson. He takes the speakers of his poems from the world of myth rather than history. The poems contain little narrative dimension, but use the character's situation to explore some extraordinary emotion. Like Tennyson, Swinburne uses the resources of sound as a narcotic and a minimal progression within the poem to depict some informing obsession shaping the speaker's world. Nonetheless, the two use the mythological narrative that they invoke to quite different effects. Tennyson frequently uses the narrative from which he takes his speakers to cast an irony over the poems that they speak. Our knowledge of the Lotos-Eaters or the "sea fairies" from the *Odyssey* gives us a perspective from which we see their persuasions as dangerous temptations. Tennyson's poems rarely alter the perspective of the stories they employ; rather they use it to control the exploration of dangerous emotion. Swinburne's dramatic monologues, on the other hand, are often deliberately revisionary. They use ther speakers—Tannhaüser in "Laus Veneris," Sappho in "Anactoria," the fourth-century Roman in "Hymn to Proserpine"—to invite the reader to share a heretical view of the proprieties of the culture that the story reflects. For Swinburne, as for Tennyson, the dramatic monologue allows poetic access to forbidden emotion, but Swinburne often casts his poems in such a way that they ask the reader to entertain the revision they pose. Like Morris, Swinburne reduces the irony that in Tennyson and Browning circumscribes the experience that the dramatic monologue depicts.

What, then, is the utility of the form for the two poets? If they no longer feel a need for the irony that Tennyson and Browning used to undercut the designs of the imagination, why not return to the poet's own voice? Morris and Swinburne do indeed write much more frequently in their own voices than Tennyson and Browning, and in so doing reflect a renewed confidence in the personal imagination, but they nonetheless deliberately and frequently separate the voice of the poem from the poet. That fact reflects a shared sense of the limitation which the personality of the contemporary poet imposed. Whether he defined himself like Morris as "the idle singer of an empty day" or like Swinburne as a "scandalous poet," his self-definition limited his poetic voice. The Romantic poet, for the most part, had confidence in the range and resonance of his personal voice. But post-Romantic poets from Tennyson and Browning through the followers of Pound and Eliot sought the escape that the dramatic monologue offered from the restrictions of voice imposed by the mere personality of the poet.

Literary historians have often analyzed the burden which personality imposes on the post-Romantic poet.[19] There was a growing conviction throughout the century, reflected in Tennyson's and Browning's dramatic monologues, that the self can know nothing but its own experiences. In the conclusion to *The Renaissance,* Pater articulates the fear that underlies much Victorian poetry when he writes that experience

> is ringed round for each one of us by that thick wall of personality through which no real voice has ever pierced on its way to us, or from us to that which we can only conjecture to be without. Every one of those impressions is the impression of the individual in his isolation, each mind keeping as a solitary prisoner its own dream of a world.[20]

The growing fear of a solipsism in which each mind keeps "as a solitary prisoner its own dream of a world" poses difficult problems for poetry. If man can know nothing but his own experience, if personality composes a barrier between the self and the world, the very self-consciousness which had been for the Romantics the source of poetry's divine truth became for later poets the burden which limited its significance to incommunicable personal impressions.

Increasing the writer's sense of isolation was his alienation from society as a whole. A large number of historical forces—the growing prestige of science, the increasing emphasis on material production, the growing consciousness of class conflict, to name just a few—created an increasing confusion about the ideological function of art. Artists reflected this confusion in the difficulty they had in finding an appropriate public voice. As if to compensate for the uneasiness with which they assumed a public voice, Tennyson and Browning create the many private voices of the dramatic monologue. Writers of the generation of Morris and Swinburne far more openly admit their alienation. They cultivate the role of a bohemian, but in so doing they commit themselves to a specific personality which limits the experience and the resonance to which their art could lay claim. The dramatic monologue gives the poet access to emotions and experiences his public role precludes.

Although the use which Victorian poets make of the dramatic monologue implies a discomfort with both a public and a personal voice, it is not until the end of the century in the writing of Oscar Wilde that Victorian poetics contains any systematic exposition of the social and artistic function of the mask. In his doctrine of the mask, Oscar Wilde shows how the artist's alienation motivates him to speak with voices other than his own. The mask for Wilde enables the artist to escape both the vulgarity of the specific civilization in which he finds himself and the constraints and imperfections of life itself. By cultivating a pose, the artist rebels against the restrictions of society and nature. But any one pose carries the danger of rigidification and of impoverishment of experience. Wilde shares Pater's sense that only by "a quickened, multiplied consciousness" can we resist the awful brevity of our experience.[21] Therefore, we cultivate a variety of masks: "What we call insincerity is simply a method by which we multiply our personalities."[22] The mask allows man to escape the limits of a single personality and achieve insofar as he can the intensity and stability of an aesthetic object. It paradoxically resists both the mutability and the monotony with which life limits experience.

Wilde's concept of the mask shows a number of shifts in emphasis from Browning's and Tennyson's development of the dramatic monologue. What was an implicit emphasis in Tennyson and Browning upon objectivity and freedom from the limitations of a single poetic voice becomes in Wilde an explicit program for life as well as for art. Wilde does not emphasize the separation between the man and his work that for Tennyson and Browning constituted the chief advantage of the dramatic monologue. Rather, he insists on the connection between the man and his masks. While Tennyson and Browning used the dramatic monologue both to express and evade the limitation of personality, Wilde uses the concept of the mask to transcend it. He emphasizes not the poet's distance from his voices, but the experience those voices allow him to encompass. In his concept of the mask, he turns the potential implicit in Browning's and Tennyson's multiplication of poetic voices into a solution to the very problem that had motivated the multiplication. In recommending the mask to the artist, Wilde makes explicit as well the uneasiness with contemporary society that had in part motivated Tennyson's and Browning's monologues. What had been covert discomfort with society became explicit opposition to it.

Wilde's conception of the mask strikingly anticipates Modernist poetics. Modernist poets take a poetic form predominant in Victorian poetry and develop from it a systematic concept of voice which enables them at once to express and transcend the restriction which individual personality imposes and the historical and individual particularity which any poem possesses. Like Wilde, Modernist poets make of the concept of voice not merely a poetic strategy but an idea of personality that motivates poetic expression. In this, they develop the radical implications of Victorian poetic practice. Yeats, Pound, and Eliot each use an idea of persona to contain contradictions similar to those which the dramatic monologue expresses in Victorian poetry. The idea of persona enables them to maintain a fluid and shifting relationship both between the specificity of the historical and personal situation which the poem presents and the generality to which it aspires. Because the poem is a performance, a dramatic event, the poet frees himself from any commitment to more than the occasion itself. Yet, just as the particular poem need not mean anything beyond its own experience, neither does it preclude more universal meaning. The concept of mask, of persona, of voice—to use the terms of Yeats, Pound, and Eliot, respectively—thus allows them to contain pressures toward the definition and the expansion of personality, the specificity and generality of statement, self-concealment, and self-expression.[23] These conflicts are the very ones which the Romantics depended upon the category of the imagination to resolve. The major Victorian and Modernist poets, with the important exception of Yeats, seek to avoid making the personal agency which imagination involves a central category of their poetics. Yeats evolves a conception of the mask which stresses its dynamic relationship with will and imagination. Eliot and Pound, more similar than Yeats to the Victorians in this regard, depend far more heavily upon the way in which the concept of persona enables them to avoid the poet's personal agency and to contain without confronting central tensions of their poetic enterprise.

Unlike Pound and Eliot, Yeats wrote a considerable amount of poetry based on the ideal of personal utterance before he developed his doctrine of the mask. His evolution therefore allows us to see the specific problems which the idea of the mask enabled him to solve. In his autobiography, Yeats recounts an incident in his early life that motivated him to write a poetry which expresses man's emotions exactly as he experiences them. Idly reading a newspaper, he comes upon some verses written by a political exile who had died a few days after returning to Ireland. Although badly written, they move him profoundly because

> they contained the actual thoughts of a man at a passionate moment of life, and when I met my father I was full of the discovery. We should write out our own thoughts in as nearly as possible the language we thought them in, as though in a letter to an intimate friend. We should not disguise them in any way; for our lives give them force as the lives of people in plays give force to their words.

After describing his father's objections to this "egotism," Yeats continues:

> I tried from then on to write out of my emotions exactly as they came to me in life, not changing them to make them more beautiful. "If I can be sincere and make my language natural, and without becoming discursive, like a novelist,

and so indiscreet and prosaic," I said to myself, "I shall, if good luck or bad luck make my life interesting, be a great poet; for it will be no longer a matter of literature at all."[24]

In rereading those early poems, Yeats criticizes their "romantic convention" and their "unconscious drama," but he ultimately finds in his early poetry not merely a problem of poetic realization but one of aesthetic principle. The poetics of sincerity upon which he bases his early work puts an unbearable pressure upon the poet to sustain experience at the necessary intensity. And a great poet needs the "good luck" which makes his life interesting. Furthermore, any specific personality limits the range of subjects and attitudes that the poet can explore. Even more burdensome to Yeats than the restriction which any personal voice imposes, however, is the way in which the pressure toward Romantic originality keeps him from achieving the common voice which he reveres. In the introduction to his work that he wrote late in his life, Yeats describes his early intuition that he had to escape the limitations of Romantic egoism.

> I read nothing but romantic literature; hated that dry eighteenth-century rhetoric; but they had one quality I admired and admire: they were not separated individual men; they spoke or tried to speak out of a people to a people; behind them stretched the generations. I knew, though but now and then as young men know things, that I must turn from that modern literature Jonathan Swift compared to the web a spider draws out of its bowels; I hated and still hate with an ever growing hatred the literature of the point of view. I wanted, if my ignorance permitted, to get back to Homer, to those that fed at his table. I wanted to cry as all men cried, to laugh as all men laughed.[25]

The concept that allows Yeats to transcend the "literature of the point of view" is the mask. Yeats writes that his mind began "drifting vaguely towards that doctrine" in the section of his autobiography concerning the years 1887–91.[26] Ellmann places Yeats's significant development of the concept in the first years of the twentieth century, coincident with his reading of Nietzsche.[27] Yeats's most systematic exposition of the concept occurs in *Per Amica Silentia Lunae* (1917) and *A Vision* (1925). As Yeats develops his idea of the mask, he moves from a conception that emphasizes the escape that the mask enables from a present which inhibits poetic energy to one that places the mask as an element in a systematic model of personality which paradoxically offers both unity and multiplicity of being. In his earlier descriptions of the mask, Yeats attributes to it the power to transcend the limitations that both the modern age and the individual self place upon emotional and poetic realization. Like Wilde, Yeats specifically relates the mask to the pressure of alienation with which a vulgar and materialistic age afflicts the artist. In an extract from a diary that he kept in 1909, he writes: "Style, personality—deliberately adopted and therefore a mask—is the only escape from the hot-faced bargainers and the money-changers."[28] But the mask for Yeats is not merely an escape. As the following passage demonstrates, the mask releases an energy inhibited by the present.

> My mind began drifting vaguely towards that doctrine of "the mask" which has convinced me that every passionate man (I have nothing to do with mechanist, or philanthropist, or man whose eyes have no preference) is, as it were, linked with another age, historical or imaginary, where alone he finds images that rouse his energy.[29]

Yeats feels that the present age inhibits energy for a number of related reasons. The alienation which the artist experiences involves him in constant reaction to a hostile environment rather than in the action Yeats prizes. Furthermore, the effort at original self-realization which modern literature encourages makes man gentle and passive. In "Ego Dominus Tuus," Hic seeks to "find myself and not an image." Ille replies:

> That is our modern hope, and by its light
> We have lit upon the gentle, sensitive mind
> And lost the old nonchalance of the hand.

The mask offered Yeats freedom from the pain of introspection, access to a spontaneous heroic energy. He writes in a diary entry which he later quotes in *Per Amica Silentia Lunae*:

> I think that all happiness depends on the energy to assume the mask of some other self; that all joyous or creative life is a re-birth as something not oneself, something

which has no memory and is created in a moment and perpetually renewed. We put on a grotesque or solemn
painted face to hide us from the terrors of judgment, in-
vent an imaginative Saturnalia where one forgets reality, a
game like that of a child, where one loses the infinite pain
of self-realization. Perhaps all the sins and energies of the
world are but its flight from an infinite blinding beam.[30]

This passage shows the way in which Yeats diverges from the
Romantic tradition. He associates self-realization with "infinite
pain." He seeks rebirth as "something not oneself, something
which has no memory and is created in a moment and perpetually
renewed." Robert Langbaum has argued that Yeats revises the
expressive theory upon which Romantic poetry is based by insisting that poetry expresses not the struggle toward some uniquely
individual self but the struggle to incorporate an external image,
"the mask of some other self."[31] The struggle is a tragic one
because man can never become the image of his desire. But his
power to release the energy of that desire depends upon his
ability to imagine his mask.

Despite the way in which Yeats revises the expressive ideal of
Romantic poetics, he seeks in the mask access to some ultimate
self. Although Yeats uses the term "mask" in his writing with all
its various implications of role, concealment, defensive armor, as
Ellmann's work demonstrates,[32] he defines the mask in his systematic criticism as the antiself, the image of character which
contains the qualities the individual most lacks and wishes to incorporate. The mask thus consists of a motivating ideal which
always exists in tension with a man's given personality; yet man
can only envision unity of being in the struggle to embrace the
mask. As Yeats develops his conception of the mask, he increasingly seeks to give it the sanction of some supernatural
agency. *Per Amica Silentia Lunae* envisions man's quarrel with
himself as an ordained vision from a supernatural opposite or
daimon who is paradoxically an ultimate self. *A Vision* places
even more stress upon the supernatural ordination of man and
his mask. *A Vision* also gives the mask greater multiplicity. In *Per
Amica Silentia Lunae,* Yeats defines only self and mask; in *A Vision*
he distinguishes between not only a true and a false mask but
twenty-eight phases of personality with their concomitant true
and false masks, wills, creative minds, and bodies of fate. By
combining the supernatural ordination of a model of person-

ality with the multiplicity of its historical incarnations, Yeats resolves the problem with which an introspective poetics had confronted him. The model allows all particular personalities to manifest some phase of ultimate being, while the particular incarnations give access to a multiplicity of psychological states. The mask thus accomplishes the task that Yeats had first envisioned for it. It sustains his claims to an authentic self, while it removes the limitation which the introspective contemplation of some uniquely individual self seemed to impose upon the poet.

The advantages that the theory of the mask holds for Yeats's poetry thus in part resemble those contained for Tennyson and Browning in the dramatic monologue, but the mask enables Yeats to claim as well the unity of being so central to Romantic poetics. The mask gives Yeats access to emotions or states of being which he felt his personality could not encompass, and it allows those states of being an objective status, even a supernatural authority. Yet Yeats's theory of the mask ultimately gives a more complex answer to the problem of personality's limitation than do Tennyson's and Browning's dramatic monologues. Tennyson and Browning both sought to evade confronting the relationship of the poet to his masks. They both repeatedly stressed the separation of the poetic voices they created from themselves. The dramatic monologue as a form permits that separation. The theory of the mask allows Yeats not only the license to speak through voices seemingly more objective than his personal speaking voice but a theory connecting those voices to his own personality. The theory of personality that Yeats develops from the image of the mask allows him to objectify and dramatize not merely characters separate from the self but a conception of psychology that unites the self to its opposite. The mask associates the personality with a range of eternal archetypes in which the individual participates and from which poetry takes universality and objectivity.

Although Yeats writes many poems from the beginning of his career for dramatic characters like King Goll, Moll Magee, or Fergus and the Druid, he first tries to objectify his own lyrical utterance in *The Wind Among the Reeds.* Many of the titles of poems in this volume strive to give a dramatic objective status to what would otherwise be a personal lyric which we would refer to the poet's own experience. Titles like "The Lover Tells of the Rose in his Heart," "The Lover Mourns for the Loss of Love,"

"He Bids his Beloved Be At Peace," "The Lover asks Forgiveness because of his Many Moods" make the reader approach the lyric statement of the poem as the statement of a character or aspect of character that the poet has objectively distanced and separated from himself. It is striking that these poems were written in the decade from which Yeats dates his preoccupation with the mask. The changes that Yeats made in the titles suggest how conscious his purpose was. "The Lover Tells of the Rose in his Heart" was originally titled "The Rose in my Heart"; "The Lover Mourns for the Loss of Love," "Loss of Love." When Yeats first published *The Wind Among the Reeds* in 1899, he attached many of the poems to characters from "The Secret Rose." "The Rose in my Heart" became "Aedh tells of the Rose in his Heart"; "The Loss of Love" became "Aedh Mourns for the Loss of Love." When he revised the poems for the *Collected Poems* of 1906, he gave them the more generalized titles by which we now know them. The second change Yeats made in the titles suggests his continuing effort to attach the utterances of his poems to principles of mind rather than to actual personages, whether the poet or an imaginary character.[33] Throughout his poetic career, Yeats continues to write poems in which the title identifies the song as the dramatic expression of some archetypal phase of passion rather than the poet's personal utterance— "A Man Young and Old," "The Man and the Echo," "Young Man's Song," "A Drunken Man's Praise of Sobriety."

The kinship of these poems, in which the title gives dramatic objectivity to a lyric utterance, to Yeats's poems in voices quite distinct from his own—"A Woman Young and Old," the Crazy Jane poems, the "Supernatural Songs"—suggests the relationship of Yeats's theory of the mask to his creation of dramatic personae. Yeats seeks personae that like the mask can give a supernatural authority to their words and that have access to emotions with a radical purity and energy to which he could not lay claim. He chooses either speakers of universal generality—a lady, a woman, a chambermaid—or mad prophets—Crazy Jane, Tom the Lunatic, Ribh. These last poems are the most interesting because they recall the madness Tennyson and Browning often associated with the speakers of dramatic monologues, but Yeats turns that madness to very different use. Whereas Tennyson and Browning make the madness of their characters undermine the validity of their perceptions and thus certain kinds of imaginative energy, Yeats uses the madness of his speakers to criticize a world that so restricts imaginative possibility that it labels them as mad. In the Crazy Jane poems, for example, Jane's "craziness," her breaking of conventional limits, gives her an energy, a vision, a wisdom greater than that of the world which surrounds her. Yeats uses that craziness to criticize the "sane," institutionally sanctioned judgments of her antagonist, the bishop. Crazy Jane has a divine madness which only a world with the bishop's limited vision dismisses as crazy. Thus, although Yeats constructs his theory of the mask and his various dramatic personae out of a similar sense of the limitations of the poet's personal voice that motivated Tennyson and Browning in their creation of dramatic monologues, Yeats uses the mask, uses those personae, to release and espouse imaginative energy rather than to ironize and control it.

The theory of the mask and Yeats's experiments with personae contribute to his finest achievement—the lyric of multiple voice.[34] Despite the ideal value he attached to the mask, he strove to create a poetry that represented not the ideal in its purity but man's struggle toward it. In *Per Amica Silentia Lunae*, Yeats recalls a phrase, "a hollow image of fulfilled desire." He continues: "All happy art seems to me that hollow image, but when its lineaments express also the poverty or the exasperation that set its maker to work, we call it tragic art."[35] This passage articulates a tragic ideal for the lyric according to which the poet centers the poem on a tension between a personality contingent upon daily circumstances and a spiritual world of essential value. The mask provides the validation and connection to that world; the psychology that centers on man's relation to his masks provides a poetics that justifies lyrics like "Vacillation" or "Nineteen Hundred and Nineteen," where Yeats alternates oracular utterance, personal lyric, dramatic dialogue in a way that both uses and transcends personal utterance, allowing the self to participate in an objective world of eternal archetypes. In "Vacillation," for example, the title indicates its poetic mode. The alternating voices of the poem—oracular declaration, personal reminiscence and reflection, the dialogue of heart and soul—articulate the claims of various aspects of self. The gaps between sections make the reader construct whatever relationships the poem implies between the claims it voices. By constructing a lyric of multiple voices, Yeats can contain conflicts between particular circumstance and eternal vision, subject and object, self and mask without forcing their resolution. Yet in the way in which he achieves that containment, he differs from Tennyson and Browning. He makes the relationship between self and projected voice not the implicit strategy but the explicit center of his enterprise. The struggle of the self to create artifice, to discover its mask, forms the subject of Yeats's major lyric poetry.

In his project to relate personal imaginative energy to an eternal world of symbol, Yeats is essentially a Romantic. There are critics—chief among them Harold Bloom—who are impatient with Yeats's attempts to objectify, to find supernatural validation for his personal speaking voice, "to speak with more than the voice of a solitary ego."[36] Yet the sense of limitation which the poet's ego imposes has been the burden of all post-Romantic poetry. While Yeats's doctrine of the mask provides him with more than the voice of the solitary ego, it also strives to connect those voices to the ego, to release its potential imaginative energy in a way that Tennyson's and Browning's experiments with personae evade. Yeats attempts to confront a tension implicit in Victorian poetry which vitiates its achievement. That he sometimes fails by choosing the dogmatic comfort his voices offer only supports Yeats's own view of the tragic nature of the poet's enterprise.

In a passage from his journal, Yeats makes a revealing parallel between himself and Pound:

> I have felt when re-writing every poem—"The Sorrow of Love" for instance—that by assuming a self of past years, as remote from that of today as some dramatic creation, I touched a stronger passion, a greater confidence than I possess, or ever did possess. Ezra when he re-creates Propertius or some Chinese poet escapes his scepticism.[37]

Much like the ideal self which Yeats creates in the conception of the mask, historical personae enable Pound to participate in stronger, purer passions than he can express in his own voice. Like Yeats, Pound attributes the difficulty in speaking in one's own voice to an alienation from the surrounding culture. In an explanation of the origin of myth, he argues that myth arises from the need to objectify personal emotion in the face of an unbelieving audience:

The first myths arose when man walked sheer into 'non-sense,' that is to say, when some very vivid and undeniable adventure befell him, and he told someone else who called him a liar. Thereupon, after bitter experience, perceiving that no one could understand what he meant when he said that he 'turned into a tree' he made a myth—a work of art that is—an impersonal or objective story woven out of his own emotion, as the nearest equation that he was capable of putting into words.[38]

The early poem "Masks" explicitly argues that the poetic mask defends the poet from a hostile audience.

These tales of old disguisings, are they not
Strange myths of souls that found themselves among
Unwonted folk that spake an hostile tongue?[39]

Donald Davie argues that American poets feel a far more awk-ward relationship with their public than Yeats did and so assume the mask to achieve a public voice in a way significantly different from "the naturally histrionic" Irishman.[40] It is true that the difference between Pound's circumstances and his poetry seems greater than in the case of Yeats. Pound did not systematically cultivate a native idiom as Yeats did or a bardic personal voice. Nonetheless, mask serves both Pound and Yeats as a defense against those limitations which they felt the age placed upon the voice and the tradition to which the artist could lay claim. By personae, Pound could take upon himself an authority, a range of experience, a culture far beyond that which his own person-ality and culture gave him.

It is interesting to wonder whether Yeats had any influence upon Pound's development of the concept of persona. During the years of their close contact (1909–13), Yeats was much pre-occupied with the mask. But Pound himself gave generous cred-it not to Yeats but to Browning. In the review of Eliot which I quoted at the beginning of this chapter, Pound likens his interest in Eliot's poems to his interest in Browning's achievement.[41] In 1928 he wrote to René Taupin, "Und überhaupt ich stamm aus Browning. Pourquoi nier son père?"[42]

Despite Pound's tribute to Browning, Pound's critics tend to emphasize the distinctions between Browning's dramatic mono-logues and Pound's personae.[43] Of course differences exist.

Pound is not interested in the circumstantial drama in which Browning often engages his characters but in an intense moment of experience from which he eliminates all possible narrative circumstance. Furthermore, Pound does not seek to create the elaborate dramatic irony with which Browning presents his characters. Pound also associates different problems with self-consciousness. Whereas self-consciousness for Browning involves the danger of imprisoning obsession, it carries the danger for Pound of fragmentation. Even the poems of Pound that most resemble Browning's show this difference in emphasis. In "Sestina: Altaforte" and "Pierre Vidal Old," the only poems in *Personae* that concern the kind of obsessions that fascinated Browning, Pound stresses not the limitation of vision that obsession involves but the focusing intensity, the artistic coherence it affords.

Despite these differences, Browning and Pound share central epistemological assumptions that shape their poetic enterprise in similar ways. Both define the self not by external events but by moments of subjective intensity, what Browning calls "the rare flashes of momentary conviction that come and go in the habitual dusk and doubt of one's life."[44] The dramatic monologue or the dramatic lyric is the appropriate form to express such a vision of experience. In trying to explain the dramatic lyric to William Carlos Williams, Pound emphasizes just this aspect of the form.

> To me the short so-called dramatic lyric—at any rate the sort of thing I do—is the poetic part of a drama the rest of which (to me the prose part) is left to the reader's imagination or implied or set in a short note. I catch the character I happen to be interested in at the moment he interests me, usually a moment of song, self-analysis, or sudden understanding or revelation.[45]

Although Pound singled out *Men and Women* as the volume of Browning's verse to praise for formal innovation, the conception of the dramatic lyric that Pound articulates here owes much more to Browning's dramatic lyrics and romances than to the more circumstantial dramatic monologues. "Two in the Campagna," "Through the Metidja to Abd El Kadr," "A Toccata of Galuppi's" present the intense moment realized or lost much like Pound's *Personae* does.

The intense subjective apprehension which for Pound as for Browning defines reality often separates the perceiver from an objective context and from a surrounding social world. Pound's explanations of myth and mask which I quoted above show him particularly sensitive to the isolation which results from such visionary experiences. Like Browning, Pound as a poet aspires to a social and historical connectedness and an objectivity greater than subjective apprehension seems to afford. The historically located dramatic lyric provides Pound, like Browning, a way containing the tension between the value he places on subjective perception and the objectivity to which he aspires as a poet. By becoming the anonymous maker or the scholarly retriever of subjective texts, Pound bestows on subjective perception the historical connection and the objective validity to which he aspires. As historically located texts on the pages of a book, his poems provide objective evidence of historical reality at one and the same time as they record a personal vision. As readers, we at once experience the subjective apprehension that defines reality for a Bertrans, a Pierre Vidal, a seafarer, while we have the text which allows us access to a historical moment. Because such texts compose events, not statements, they avoid the burden of telling truth; they are truth. Pound, like Browning, uses the dramatic lyric, located at a moment in history, to mediate between the subjective and the objective. Historical and literary personae allow him to give objectivity to personal utterance.

The way in which the form of the dramatic lyric functions to objectify subjective experience explains Pound's fascination in *Personae* with the transformation of self into artifact. Like Browning's dramatic monologues, many of Pound's dramatic lyrics concern the metamorphosis of the speaker into a natural or an aesthetic object immune from the flux of time. In "La Fraisne," for example, the speaker seeks freedom from the pain of love's mutability in his metamorphosis into a tree. Similarly, in "Cino" and in "Na Audiart," the speaker transforms and transcends the failings of earthly love by changing women into "the souls of song." Although metamorphosis is as old a theme as the world's mutability, it has a particular significance for Pound because of the way in which it illuminates the formal enterprise of his poetry. The masks that Pound assumes offer aesthetic metamorphoses of the self held in tension against the flux and inchoateness of experience. Pound describes his use of the mask in just this way in a passage from *Gaudier-Brzeska*:

In the "search for oneself," in the search for "sincere self-expression," one gropes, one finds some seeming verity. One says "I am" this, that, or the other, and with the words scarcely uttered one ceases to be that thing.

I began this search for the real in a book called *Personae*, casting off, as it were, complete masks of the self in each poem. I continued in long series of translations, which were but more elaborate masks.[46]

The mask saves some aspect of the self from the destructive power of time by providing both an external correlative and an aesthetic metamorphosis. But even at the moment of transformation, "one ceases to be that thing." The mask thus exists in constant tension with an identity which is multiple, inchoate, constantly shifting. Like Browning, like Yeats, Pound satisfies a need for permanence by crafting the particular mask, while he remains true to the flux of experience by the process of casting off masks in each poem. Pound's quest in his poetry resembles the quest of individual personae in their metamorphoses of self. Not only the speakers of Pound's poems but the genre itself explores the self's potential to objectify in face of the flux and multiplicity of experience.

In the course of his development, Pound allows increasing fluidity to the relationship between the mask and the stance of the poet.[47] While Pound's early poems dramatize the experience of a single, historically located speaker, his later poetry often takes as its subject the poet's imagination of himself as a persona. *Hugh Selwyn Mauberley* provides the best example of this subject outside of *The Cantos*. One of the greatest problems with which the poem confronts its readers is the difficulty of defining the precise boundaries of Mauberley as a character in relationship to Pound.[48] This very difficulty suggests the enterprise of the poem. In Mauberley Pound presents not a distinctly delineated character but the project of imagining oneself as a character. The title of the first section, "E. P. Ode pour l'election de son sepulchre," suggests the relationship of Mauberley to Pound. Mauberley is in some sense Pound's tomb, an artifact cast and projected from the self and serving both as living memorial and acknowledgment of separation and departure. Yet even the seeming clarity of that relationship becomes unstable in the course of the poem. We begin the poem by describing a "he," that we assume to be Mauberley, who is distinct from the narrating I of the poem, that we assume to be Pound. Yet as Pound proceeds to describe the society that Mauberley inhabits, in sections like "Sienna Mi Fe" or "Mr. Nixon," he increasingly presents himself as an actor in that world that can be identified with Mauberley. As the narrating I becomes more prominent, the relationship between Mauberley and Pound becomes more unstable. As if to contain this instability, Pound recapitulates the poem's major themes in the section headed "Mauberley (1920)" with a narrative of Mauberley's career that presents him as an individual distinct from Pound. Yet the way in which the first part of the poem has derived the character of Mauberley from Pound's experience allows us to see this second major section of the poem only as a more clearly distinguished projection. Mauberley finally speaks in the poem only after he dies. An oar cast up on the beach reads

> "I was
> "And I no more exist;
> "Here drifted
> "An hedonist."

Like Pound, Mauberley speaks only his epitaph. The self recognizes the shape of its experience in a projection, a mask, that acknowledges that one has ceased to be that thing. Like Browning's bishop of St. Praxed's church, Pound memorializes his personae in an epitaphic poetry.

Hugh Selwyn Mauberley ends with a lyric, "Medallion," which most readers identify as Mauberley's. It thus resembles Pound's earlier persona poems, a lyric given historical and psychological location in the naming of the persona who speaks it. Yet the complex and unstable poem that precedes it makes the interpretation of that final lyric a far more difficult act than the surface difficulty of the lyric suggests, for the persona lacks the clarity or stability of definition of Pound's earlier speakers. This very instability suggests the poem's accomplishment. In *Mauberley,* Pound discovers a way of showing the interchange between poet and persona. He creates a poem whose focus is the fluidity of relationship between mask and poet, subjective and objective, self-concealment and self-dramatization. Pound's evolution of persona thus in some ways resembles Yeats's evolution of the idea of the mask. Pound initially finds in persona a strategy that releases a poetic energy inhibited by various contemporary constraints. Like Yeats, he develops persona to reflect a complex, dynamic interchange between the self and its projections. Unlike Yeats, however, Pound does not have a conception of unity of being that gives the struggle both its ideal resolution and its tragedy. Rather Pound simply locates the tension within the field of the poem. He thus can write poems about personal voice which claim for their achievement the construction of an impersonal medium within which they contain subject and object, man and mask, sustained in the flux which is experience. Such a conception of the poetic enterprise runs the risk of finally providing no coherent center. Much like Browning, Pound would like to assume that a center materializes from its circumference. If that center does not materialize, identity consists in a collection of historical debris, of flotsam without a cohering principle. Much as Mr. Sludge provides a negative image of identity for Browning. "Portrait D'Une Femme" provides one for Pound. The self has no more coherence and originality than the bric-a-brac of its hoarding: "Nothing that's quite your own. / Yet this is you."

As Pound observes in his review of T. S. Eliot's first volume of poems, Eliot writes much of his early poetry in the form of the dramatic monologue. "The Love Song of J. Alfred Prufrock," "Portrait of a Lady," "Gerontion," "The Hollow Men" all represent the perceptions of a speaker distinct from the poet. Even the voices of *The Waste Land* were conceived as dramatic characters; its original title was "He do the police in different voices." Like Tennyson and Browning, Eliot uses the dramatic monologue to explore man's imprisonment within his own consciousness. Phenomena in the early poems exist only as the reflex of the perceiving self; other people cannot see that self as it really is. In the notes to *The Waste Land,* Eliot quotes a passage from F. H. Bradley which could well stand as an epigraph to his early poetry.

My external sensations are no less private to myself than are my thoughts or my feelings. In either case my experience falls within my own circle, a circle closed on the outside; and, with all its elements alike, every sphere is opaque to the others which surround it. . . . In brief, regarded as

an existence which appears in a soul, the whole world for
each is peculiar and private to that soul.

This quotation from Bradley recalls the passage from the conclusion to *The Renaissance* which I quoted above. Experience, re-
duced to a group of impressions, is ringed round "by that thick
wall of personality through which no real voice has ever pierced
on its way to us, or from us to that which we can only conjecture
to be without."

Although Eliot credited Browning with the invention of the
dramatic monologue, his own monologues resemble Tennyson's
rather than Browning's. Like Tennyson, Eliot exploits the resonance of myth to give the phases of private passion which interested him a range of universal associations. Like Tennyson,
Eliot is less interested in creating particular historical characters
than in using character to delimit a zone of consciousness.
Gerontion and Tiresias are names with which Eliot associates
perceptions which have not been sharply individuated. Again
like Tennyson, Eliot makes little use of narrative. Eliot's poems
rarely contain clearly defined events. Eliot could well be describing his own poetry when he remarks of Tennyson that he uses
narrative situation only as the occasion for "stating an elegiac
mood."[49]

The elegiac moods which Tennyson's and Eliot's poems express display remarkably similar patterns. Like Tennyson, unlike Browning, Eliot does not engage his characters in mad
projections of the will to control the world. Rather, his characters doubt that there can be meaningful interchange between
the world and the self. Prufrock fears that any gesture to engage
another runs the risk of misunderstanding the other's desires:
"That is not what I meant at all. That is not it, at all." Gerontion
refuses intimacy because he is convinced of his own impotence:
"I have lost my sight, smell, hearing, taste and touch: How
should I use them for your closer contact?" The hollow men
dare not meet the eyes of others who have crossed to death's
other kingdom because of their own failure. In the monologue,
the speaker laments his loss while he constructs a fiction of the
self that at once rationalizes his failure and consoles him for it. J.
Alfred Prufrock tells himself that he is no prophet, no Prince
Hamlet, but an attendant lord, a fool, who never could have
forced the moment to its crisis. The accuracy and wit of his social

satire and the plangency of his lament for his failure alike afford him defenses against the world he has refused to enter. He depicts the world as not worthy of his desires, which he subdues through the medium of nostalgia. Like the Lotos-Eaters or like Tithonus, Prufrock constructs a monologue whose fictions insulate and preserve him in a solipsistic dream world, a chamber of the sea. The poem at once mourns his loss while it defends him against the engulfment with which the world threatens him, the human voices which could only wake him to drown.

Like Tennyson, Eliot is thus very much preoccupied with the pains and indulgences of the solitary ego. The form of the dramatic monologue offers him similar resources for dealing with such emotional states. The device of specific character allows him to place a circumference around the sensibility he depicts. Like Tithonus, J. Alfred Prufrock or Gerontion gives a local habitation and a name to a diffuse collection of emotional associations while the form allows him to objectify those emotions and to ironize them. The Modernist techniques that separate Eliot from Tennyson in fact allow him to intensify the effects that Tennyson also sought to achieve. Readers have frequently noted the vagueness in the definition of setting and audience in Tennyson's dramatic monologues. Eliot quite brilliantly transforms what is sometimes a confusion of address in Tennyson's poems to a deliberately manipulated dissonance that confirms the speaker's isolation. Prufrock begins with a definite address and invitation, "Let us go then you and I," but the poem, as all readers have noticed, so deliberately avoids defining its events and audience that we question whether the poem records any interchange with a world external to the speaker's consciousness. In order to depict the isolation of that consciousness, Eliot combines two modes that Tennyson uses independently to present his characters' alienation: the social satire of poems like *Maud* or "Locksley Hall" and the mythological resonance of "Tithonus" or "Ulysses." The characteristic voice of Eliot's early monologues results in part from his combination of those registers. As different as that voice is from Tennyson's, it depicts a similar subject—the burden of personality.

It is not a surprising paradox that Eliot's preoccupation with the burden of personality exists in the context of a poetics strenuous in its efforts to dissociate the category of personality from the poet. "Tradition and the Individual Talent" contains the fullest discussion of this dissociation. In that essay, Eliot defines the progress of the artist as "a continual self-sacrifice, a continual extinction of personality."[50] Eliot can describe the artist in this way by refusing to attribute agency to what Romantic poets and theorists would call the imagination. The poet's mind is "a more finely perfected medium," "a receptacle for seizing and storing up numberless feelings, phrases, images."[51] It is the shred of platinum which provides the catalyst for a chemical combination in which it is unaffected. Eliot attributes agency in a rather oblique way to the feelings stored in the medium of the poet's mind. He writes that these feelings "are at liberty to enter into new combinations"; that they remain in the mind "until all the particles which can unite to form a new compound are present together."[52] Even these formulations avoid the deliberate choice that would imply a specific actor. The chemical metaphor allows Eliot to avoid the category of agency; the reaction just happens when the appropriate materials are present.

There is a striking parallel between the avoidance of action in Eliot's poetry and the avoidance of agency in his criticism, although they express opposing impulses. Characters in Eliot's poetry like Prufrock or the hollow men avoid acting out of a crippling sense of personality, whereas Eliot's criticism avoids agency to escape the category of personality. Eliot himself implies the relationship in a passage from "Tradition and the Individual Talent":

> Poetry is not a turning loose of emotion, but an escape from emotion; it is not the expression of personality, but an escape from personality. But, of course, only those who have personality and emotions know what it means to want to escape from these things.[53]

The device of persona allows Eliot to express the burden of personality and to dissociate that burden from the poet. He thus strives to shift attention from the poet to the poem. The poem can control, delimit, and objectify what the poet finds so burdensome.

Eliot's theory of impersonality lies far less comfortably with his poetry than Yeats's and Pound's theories of mask and persona do with their work. Unlike Yeats, he strives to evade the connection between "the man who suffers and the mind which creates."[54] Unlike Pound, Eliot makes his characteristic subject the solipsism which the category of personality involves. Furthermore, he does not develop a way of locating the tension between poet and persona within the field of the poem as Pound does. As a result, Eliot's work contains a far greater conflict between the burden of personality which his poems concern and the impersonality to which the poet lays claim. In his preoccupation with the solipsism of the individual imagination and in his evasion of the connection between a poet and his personae, Eliot is the closest of the principal Modernist poets to the Victorian poetic tradition. Like Browning and Tennyson, he uses the dramatic monologue to express a fear that self-consciousness, far from offering the access to universals which the Romantic hoped, confirms the reality of man's self-imprisonment. Like Browning and Tennyson again, Eliot strives to dissociate the personality of the poet from the poem. Like the Victorians, Eliot uses the dramatic monologue out of a conviction that a poem is inevitably a personal utterance and out of a desire to give a poem the qualities of an object that transcends the condition of human speech. The poem does not resolve the tension; it contains it within the experience of the text.

Eliot and Pound have given modern critical theory many of its terms and assumptions. Although the concept of persona did not come into wide usage until the 1950s,[55] it owes its modern critical revival in large part to Pound. In his 1953 essay "The Three Voices of Poetry," T. S. Eliot gives credit to "Browning's greatest disciple, Mr. Ezra Pound, for adopting the term persona to indicate the historical or fictional mask a poet may assume to address his audience."[56] Although Eliot limits the use of the term to poems which we would refer to as dramatic monologues, his insistence elsewhere on separating the personality of the poet from the poem has influenced the term's broader application to the speakers of all poems. Use of the term persona for the speaker of any poem results in part from the New Criticism's attempt to eliminate statements of intentionality from the analysis of poetry. In this attempt, current use of the term shows a tension similar to the one I have located in Victorian and modern poetry, between acknowledging certain modern problems of personality and objectifying them in art. On the one hand, the term persona implies not a single sense of identity, the sincere man talking to men of Romantic critical theory, but a multiple, fragmented sense of identity which is relative to particular occasions. On the other hand, the term persona also attempts to delimit and objectify such a conception of identity. It seeks to avoid both the category of personality and the logical incongruity into which the New Criticism often falls of attributing to objects qualities of agency which are appropriate only to persons.[57] The term persona recognizes issues of identity and personality that inevitably impose themselves on literature while it seeks to give those issues the control, the limitation, and the objectivity of the work of art.[58]

Eliot's, Yeats's and Pound's preoccupation with mask and persona typifies many of the poets who follow them. Frost, Jarrell, Tate, and Lowell write extensively in the dramatic monologue. Other poets create personae—William Carlos Williams's Paterson, John Berryman's Henry, Charles Olson's Maximus—that enable them to manipulate a more outrageous personality than their own while maintaining an irony, an ambivalence, toward the words of that character.[59] Even a poet like Wallace Stevens, who firmly grounds his poetry in the I of the poet, hesitates to use the proper pronominal voice.[60] In the last two decades, however, a number of poets and critics have rejected the idea of persona. The change in Robert Lowell's poetry with the volume *Life Studies* emblemizes many contemporary poets' rejection of elaborate personae for a personal confessional voice. In his essay "On Sincerity," Donald Davie asserts the significance of this new Romanticism:

> We must be glad to be compelled to recognize that we are all, like it or not, post-Romantic people; that the historical developments which we label "Romanticism" were not a series of aberrations which we can and should disown, but rather a sort of landslide which permanently transformed the landscape of the 20th century we inhabit, however reluctantly.[61]

The poets who have been the subjects of this chapter all tried in various ways to transform what Davie calls the landslide that was the heritage of Romanticism. Nonetheless, we must qualify Davie's argument. Although the search for impersonality of many Victorian and Modernist poets appeared to them—and to many of their critics—as a rejection of Romanticism, the very way in which they conceive of dramatic monologue, mask, and persona puts the Romantic concern with self-consciousness and its transformation into art at the very center of their poetry. The difficulty of sustaining the categories "impersonality" and "sincerity" that frequently enter post-Romantic debates about persona, suggests that they describe not alternatives but elements of a tension important to all nineteenth- and twentieth-century literature. The Victorians and the Modernists sought to contain this tension in similar ways. Even their polemical representation of Romanticism helped them maintain a precarious balance between the burden of personality that their poetry so often concerned and the escape from mere subjectivity through personality made art.

3

The Picturesque and Modernist Theories of the Image

Modern poets define their distance from the Victorians by criticizing the relationship between image and idea in Victorian poetry. In a 1936 broadcast, Yeats explains the anti-Victorianism of his generation as an attempt to rid poetry of the "psychology, science, moral fervour"[1] that diluted the work of Swinburne, Tennyson, Arnold, and Browning. In his essay "The Metaphysical Poets," Eliot criticizes the Victorians for a dissociation of thought and feeling.[2] In one of his essays defining imagism, Pound complains that the Victorians made poetry "the ox-cart and post-chaise for transmitting thoughts poetic or otherwise."[3] The ideal against which all three poets measure the achievement of the Victorians is a nondiscursive poetry of the image. Yeats calls it pure poetry.[4] Eliot calls it "direct sensuous apprehension of thought."[5] Pound calls it "an intellectual and emotional complex in an instant of time."[6] These three definitions have in common the insistence that ideas as ideas have no place in poetry, that poetry presents images that are themselves their meaning. The poets claim varied precedents for their ideal—Catullus, the metaphysicals, the troubadours, the Chinese poetic tradition. Subsequent criticism has tended to locate their most important precedent in French symbolism. In this chapter, I will argue that Modernist theories of the image also have a precedent in what Arthur Hallam, in a review of Tennyson's early poems, calls the "picturesque."[7] Hallam's review provides terms by which we can understand Tennyson's early poetic achievement, and critics have frequently taken it as an important statement of Victorian poetics.[8] But the essay also enables us to see the continuity between the Victorian and modern use of poetic objects. Hallam titles his review "On Some of the Characteristics of Modern Poetry." His attempt to define the ways in which modern poetry presents images made Yeats call the essay "fundamental and radical."[9] Yeats claimed that his own early poetry was based on Hallam's principles;[10] in more recent years Marshall McLuhan has argued that Hallam's definition of the picturesque anticipates the symbolist aesthetic.[11] Indeed, as McLuhan argues, the essay contains the ingredients for a sophisticated conception of the symbol not unlike the complex of ideas that was to develop in French poetry years later. But the essay finally stops short of such a conception, and neither Victorian poetry nor criticism ever arrives at it because of a desire to establish an objective basis for the correlation between images and feelings. The poetics of Eliot and Pound, and in a far more complicated and ambiguous way that of Yeats, also display this desire. The attempt to discover a permanent realm of symbols, objective correlatives, "equations for the human emotions"[12] separates all three poets from the French symbolists and links them to an objectivist strain central to Victorian aesthetics. Both Victorian and Modernist poetics contain theories of the image which claim objective validation for the connection between image and emotion.

Hallam bases his definition of the picturesque on a reading of literary history strikingly similar to Eliot's theory of the dissociation of sensibility.[13] Hallam writes that after the Renaissance,

> those different powers of poetic disposition, the energies of Sensitive, of Reflective, of Passionate Emotion, which in former times were intermingled, and derived from mutual support an extensive empire over the feelings of men, were now restrained within separate spheres of agency. The whole system no longer worked harmoniously, and by intrinsic harmony acquired external freedom; but there arose a violent and unusual action in the several component functions, each for itself, all striving to reproduce the regular power which the whole had once enjoyed.[14]

In *Romantic Image,* Frank Kermode argues that Eliot's theory of dissociation of sensibility validates a nondiscursive, symbolist poetics of the image by creating a myth of a golden age in which there was neither rationalist nor naturalist assault on poetry and belief.[15] The history that Hallam constructs functions in a similar way. It justifies the elimination of intellectual discourse from a poetry of images whose effect is "a sort of magic, producing a number of impressions, too multiplied, too minute, and too diversified to allow of our tracing them to their causes."[16]

Hallam calls this kind of poetry both a poetry of sensation and the picturesque. He opposes it to a poetry of reflection, which he identifies with Wordsworth. The first modern poets of sensation were Shelley and Keats. Hallam describes the operation of the peculiar poetic mind that each possessed:

> Susceptible of the slightest impulse from external nature, their fine organs trembled into emotion at colors, and sounds, and movements, unperceived or unregarded by duller temperaments. Rich and clear were their perceptions of visible forms; full and deep their feelings of music. So vivid was the delight attending the simple exertions of eye and ear, that it became mingled more and more with their trains of active thought, and tended to absorb their whole being into the energy of sense. Other poets *seek* for images to illustrate their conceptions; these men had no need to seek; they lived in a world of images; for the most important and extensive portion of their life consisted in those emotions which are immediately conversant with the sensation. . . . Hence, they are not descriptive, they are picturesque.[17]

Hallam's essay looks back to Keats and presages Eliot. Eliot's phrases—"direct sensuous apprehension of thought," the quality "of transmuting ideas into sensations, of transforming a sensation into a state of mind"—articulate a poetic ideal similar to Hallam's.[18] It is true that Hallam and Eliot construct the history which justifies their aesthetic somewhat differently. Hallam embraces the poetry of sensation that he identifies with Keats and Shelley; Eliot feels that a poetry of sensation reflects our fall from a unified sensibility. But Eliot locates the only effort of the previous century to overcome the division of thought and feeling in Keats and Shelley, and he describes the poetry of unified sensibility in a way remarkably similar to Hallam's picturesque. Both Hallam and Eliot want a nondiscursive poetry in which the juxtaposition of images alone recreates for poet and reader a complex poetic emotion inarticulable by any other means.

As McLuhan argues, Hallam's essay strikingly anticipates a symbolist aesthetic according to which poetry evokes a precise yet indefinable emotion by juxtaposing images without discursive connection. Unlike the symbolists, however, Hallam never clearly indicates whether the poet's emotion informs the objects of the external world or results from the real properties of objects. Much of the essay seems to imply a synthesizing Romantic conception of the imagination like that on which symbolism depends. But at times Hallam speaks as if the world carries within itself the objective grounds for the poet's emotion. In the passage quoted above, in which Hallam defines poetry as "a sort of magic, producing a number of impressions, too multiplied, too minute, and too diversified to allow of our tracing them to their causes," he accounts for the magic by asserting "just such was the effect, even so boundless and so bewildering, produced on their imaginations by the real appearance of Nature."[19] In enumerating the distinctive excellencies of Tennyson's poetry, Hallam first praises "his power of embodying himself in ideal characters, or rather moods of character, with such extreme accuracy of adjustment, that the circumstances of the narration seem to have a natural correspondence with the predominant feeling, and, as it were, to be evolved from it by assimilative force." Hallam's praise implies that the poet's emotion informs the objects of his landscape. In the next sentence, however, Hallam begins from the objects and works back to the emotion. He praises Tennyson's "vivid, picturesque delineation of objects, and the peculiar skill with which he holds all of them *fused,* to borrow a metaphor from science, in a medium of strong emotion."[20] Isobel Armstrong suggests that in this reversal of his first formulation Hallam uses accuracy of natural description to provide a check against the subjectivity implied in the first statement.[21]

Hallam also guards against the subjectivity that the picturesque seems to imply by basing his theory on an associational psychology grounded in physiological organization. The emotions of the poet follow "a regular law of association." "Every bosom contains the elements of those complex emotions which the artist feels, and every head can, to a certain extent, go over in itself the process of their combination, so as to understand his expressions and sympathize with his state." Hallam goes on to explain that this requires an exertion which many readers are unwilling to make. "For very many, therefore, it has become *morally* impossible to attain the author's point of vision, on account of their habits, or their prejudices, or their circumstances;

but it is never *physically* impossible, because nature has placed in every man the simple elements, of which art is the sublimation."[22]

It might be argued that the ambiguity in Hallam's location of the grounds for poetic emotion and his dependence upon a universal physiological law of association imply a Romantic theory of correspondence between man and nature. Yet it is striking that Hallam never provides such an explanation. The essay reveres beauty, not nature. Yeats, in fact, wonders whether Hallam originated the term "aesthetic school."[23] He did not, but Yeats's attribution of the term to Hallam reflects Hallam's treatment of nature. Nature functions not as a ground for philosophical understanding, as it did for Wordsworth and Coleridge, but as a source of aesthetic emotion. Yet it is an aesthetic emotion that Hallam desires to anchor in some way in the real properties of the visible universe. Hallam thus at one and the same time implies a symbolic poetics while he remains faithful to a pictorial ideal.

Both Hallam's understanding of the potential which landscape offered to create a *paysage intérieur* and his desire to achieve some fixity for emotion in the real properties of objects anticipate central characteristics of Victorian poetry and poetics. The Victorians gradually lost the sense that there could be a fit between man's mind and nature. Victorian poetics displays two seemingly contradictory responses to this loss. On the one hand, much Victorian poetry uses landscape to evoke fleeting, lyrical, otherwise inarticulable emotions essentially independent of nature. Tennyson and the Pre-Raphaelites, for example, often anticipate the symbolist construction of *paysage intérieur* in the way in which they portray states of mind through imaginary landscapes. On the other hand, much Victorian aesthetic theory tries to fix emotions in the real properties of objects. Carlyle, Mill, Ruskin, and Arnold all instruct the poet in the steadying power which precise observation of the external world gives the portrayal of emotion. These contradictory impulses explain the strange way in which Victorian poetry often grounds its phantasmagoria in the minute description of nature. Like Marianne Moore in "Poetry," Victorian poets carefully describe the real toads in their imaginary gardens. The characteristic Victorian combination of precise observation with imaginary landscape is one which Hallam's appreciation of Tennyson first implies. It ultimately will allow us to see the continuity between Victorian poetics and modern imagism, but we will look first at Tennyson's poetry and then more generally at Victorian poetry and poetics in light of Hallam's principles.

Hallam's review provides perhaps the best description to this day of Tennyson's early poetry. The most characteristic poems in the volume use landscape in the way in which Hallam describes. They juxtapose sensations of natural objects to evoke a feeling which cannot be explained or named, but only re-experienced by retracing its combination of elements. Here, for example, are the last lines of the song "A spirit haunts the year's last hours":

> My very heart faints and my whole soul grieves
> At the moist rich smell of the rotting leaves,
>   And the breath
>   Of the fading edges of box beneath,
> And the year's last rose.
>   Heavily hangs the broad sunflower
>   Over its grave i' the earth so chilly;
>   Heavily hangs the hollyhock,
>   Heavily hangs the tiger-lily.

The poem recalls Keats's "To Autumn." Everyone would claim that the Keats is far superior to the Tennyson, but the reasons would tell us less about the respective merits of the two poets than about Tennyson's poetic enterprise. Although Keats, like Tennyson, as Hallam observes, seeks a richness of sensation in his poetry, he also strives to charge words with a richness of cognitive association. He urged Shelley "to 'load every rift' of your subject with ore."[24] Tennyson, on the other hand, frequently strives to minimize the cognitive associations that words can carry in order to create the poetry of sensation that Hallam describes. He wishes not to involve the reader in the kind of understanding or reflection that a cognitively dense verbal medium encourages but to bring the reader to re-experience that moment when sensation and emotion seem one. His poetry anticipates impressionism in striving to combine sense impressions in such a way that it captures the very moment when sensation becomes feeling.

The impressionist aim of Tennyson's early poetry explains the double aspect with which he invests natural objects. He at once describes them with a scientific exactitude that made his poetry a naturalist's textbook and uses them to evoke the feeling that is the poem's occasion. "Mariana" provides the most extraordinary example of this technique.

> With blackest moss the flower-plots
>> Were thickly crusted, one and all:
> The rusted nails fell from the knots
>> That held the pear to the gable-wall.
> The broken sheds looked sad and strange;
>> Unlifted was the clinking latch;
> Weeded and worn the ancient thatch
> Upon the lonely moated grange.

Tennyson depicts the objects of Mariana's landscape with an almost photographic accuracy—the moss on the flower plots, the nails no longer holding the pear to the wall; later in the poem, the moss surrounding the sluice, the dust in the afternoon sunbeam. Yet these details convey the desolation, the morbidity, the ennui which is Mariana's sensibility. The poem contains an ambiguity similar to the one in Hallam's essay in its location of the source of emotion. We feel that it is Mariana's perception of the landscape that the poem details, yet she actually speaks only the refrain. Tennyson achieves this extraordinary effect by not supplying any organizing intelligence in his presentation of the landscape. The poem asserts that the broken sheds "looked" sad and strange, but who is the looker? Is it Mariana? Is it the speaker? Or are the sheds so constituted that anyone passing by would think them "sad and strange"? Occasionally the poem records Mariana's perceptions. "She saw the gusty shadow sway." "She heard the night-fowl crow." But more often the verbs of the poem imply that the landscape itself acts. The nails "fell," the sluice "slept," mosses "crept." At the end of the poem, when we hear that all of the sounds did "confound her sense," Tennyson confirms the ambiguity in the location of the source of emotion that has characterized the entire poem. Are the sounds inherently confounding or does her sense make them so? Tennyson builds into the poem a blurring of subject and object that leaves ambiguous its organizing principle.

John Stuart Mill's description of Tennyson's use of landscape, which precedes a discussion of "Mariana," implies this very ambiguity I have been describing. He praises Tennyson's power "of *creating* scenery, in keeping with some state of human feeling; so fitted to it as to be the embodied symbol of it, and to summon up the state of feeling itself, with a force not to be surpassed by anything but reality."[25] Like Hallam in his praise of Tennyson, Mill first implies that the mind creates the scene it perceives. He then reverses directions, however, and makes the poetic process a kind of second to reality's power to evoke emotion. Mill's comment indicates the central ambiguity of Tennyson's poetry. Tennyson understood the ways in which objects could be used to create *paysage interiéur*, but he also strove to depict objects with a realism that would in some way anchor the feelings attached to them. A poetry of sensation both expresses and contains this central ambiguity in the location of emotion.

Many of the poems which most clearly typify Hallam's definition of the poetry of sensation bear as titles women's names. These poems, as one critic of Tennyson has put it, are a puzzle and an embarrassment to Tennyson's modern readers.[26] Why the insipid gallery of lady's-book portraits? Tennyson's concern with the phenomenology of objects, I think, provides an answer, for the women's names themselves give an idealized phenomenological center to the sense impressions that compose the poem. Here, for example, is "Claribel":

> Where Claribel low-lieth
>   The breezes pause and die,
>   Letting the rose leaves fall:
> But the solemn oak-tree sigheth,
>   Thick-leaved, ambrosial,
>   With an ancient melody
>   Of an inward agony,
> Where Claribel low-lieth.
>
> At eve the beetle boometh
>   Athwart the thicket lone:
> At noon the wild bee hummeth
>   About the mossed head stone:
> At midnight the moon cometh
>   And looketh down alone.
> Her song the lintwhite swelleth,
> The clear-voiced mavis dwelleth,
>   The callow throstle lispeth,
> The slumbrous wave outwelleth,
>   The babbling runnel crispeth
> The hollow grot replieth
>   Where Claribel low-lieth.

John Stuart Mill observed that this poem might be called "a solitary place in the wood" and gain some focus.[27] Indeed the poem defines Claribel by a series of sense impressions which make her interchangeable with the place where she low-lieth. The name is only a vague center around which to locate the sensation of place. The very ambiguity of her existence enables Tennyson to maintain an ambiguity in his location of emotion.

One might rightly object at this point that one can hardly perceive the landscape of the poem because of the way in which the poem keeps insisting upon itself as sheer sound. The callow throstle isn't the only thing that lispeth as we read. The poem is subtitled "a melody," and like many of the lady poems seems to be concerned with formal patterns of sound as much as with anything else. In praising the "Ballad of Oriana," another poem in which sound repetitions play a very large part, Hallam comments on this aspect of Tennyson's style:

> There are innumerable shades of fine emotion in the human heart, especially when the senses are keen and vigilant, which are too subtle and too rapid to admit of corresponding phrases. The understanding takes no definite note of them; how then can they leave signatures in language? Yet they exist; in plenitude of being and beauty they exist; and in music they find a medium through which they pass from heart to heart. The tone becomes the sign of the feeling; and they reciprocally suggest each other.[28]

Hallam's description of Tennyson again indicates the ways in which Tennyson approaches and diverges from a symbolist ideal. Like the symbolists, he uses the sound of language to evoke emotion inarticulable in mere words. But language, far from reconstituting itself as an absolute, as it does for the French symbolists, nevertheless still functions for Tennyson as a sign; "the tone becomes the sign of the feeling." "Sound conveys meaning where words do not." Tennyson's impressionism, as I suggested above, involves a distrust of the cognitive element of language, but implies an enormous faith in the representational power of sound.

The frequent criticism of Tennyson that he creates a purely verbal universe suggests that the music of language does not function in the way in which he desired. A. Dwight Culler has argued that two different conceptions of language exist in Tennyson's work: one, that words are poor husks of reality, abstract denotative counters generalizing upon sense experience; the other that language is a magical instrument, a means of incantation or ritual which could reveal the secret of a thing by repeating its name.[29] Both conceptions of language involve a distrust of its logical function and motivate Tennyson to minimize that function in order to evoke what he alternately conceived as a sensual or spiritual essence. Both because of and despite this attempt, he creates a world in his early poetry like that of Poe or Swinburne in which language itself, separated from its signifying function, constitutes its own essence.

Although this may be the effect of Tennyson's poetry, it is an effect completely foreign to his intention. Tennyson wants sounds, like objects, to contain within themselves the potential for their own meaning. His use of language, like his use of landscape, contains within it a tension between the power objects possess to evoke emotion and the power subjects possess to bestow emotion. It is a tension that Tennyson inherited from the Romantics. Whereas the Romantics often found that space between subject and object a rich testimony to the power of the imagination, Tennyson feared it as isolating and impoverishing. He held before himself the ideal of a poetry that could discover some objective foundation for emotion. His failures and successes are alike instructive because in many ways the twentieth-century poet's attempt to write "the poem of pure reality" resembles Tennyson's quest. Eliot, Pound, and Williams also strove to create a poetics that would place the poem in the space between subject and object without the agency of the Romantic imagination. Their rhetoric assuredly was a very different one from Tennyson's and in some ways they learned from Victorian failures, but they share the attempt with Tennyson and other Victorian poets to write a poetry of images, without discourse, that unites sensation and emotion in an aesthetic complex that has objective validation.

Tennyson lost faith in this attempt fairly early in his poetic career and sought to develop a number of poetic strategies to avoid the subjectivism and aestheticism that seemed implicit in his early poetry. One of these strategies is the dramatic monologue. By associating the subjective absorption of landscape with speakers who are either insane, like the hero of *Maud,* or who are isolated from their kind, like Tithonus, Tennyson suggests the dangers such a mode of perception implies. Tennyson's dramatic monologues are his finest achievements because the form permits him, as I argued in the first chapter, to give a dramatic objectivity to the subjective mode of his finest poetry. Another strategy on which Tennyson relies to counter the aesthetic and subjective implications of the picturesque is to frame lyrical passages within a much longer narrative and discursive poem, like *The Princess, Idylls of the King, In Memoriam,* which locates and validates the lyrical moment. These longer poems often seem disjunct because Tennyson relies upon narrative to integrate the diverse lyric and discursive modes of the poems, and the narrative dimension of the poems consequently seems strained. My argument here very much resembles Eliot's account of Tennyson's dissociation of sensibility, with this difference: Eliot and Pound, far from bringing together the two elements separated in Tennyson's work, choose an imagistic mode which resembles the picturesque. Like Tennyson in his early poetry, they want a poetry of sensation becoming emotion without discourse, and they have equivalent problems, I shall argue, in their search for some objective validation of the image. Only Yeats, I think, successfully overcame the split between subject and object that was the Victorian poetic heritage, and he did it by returning to the very things that were anathema to Eliot and Pound—discourse and a Romantic theory of the imagination. Before discussing Modernist conceptions of the image, however, I will look more generally at Victorian poetry and poetics in light of Tennyson's practice.

The split between a presymbolist subjectivism and an attempt to establish objective validation for the image that we have seen in Hallam and Tennyson runs throughout Victorian poetry and poetics. Much Victorian poetic theory concerns the connection between feeling and seeing. Unlike Romantic poetic theory, however, it tries to establish a right connection between the two, so that seeing the object appropriately, "as it really is," automatically produces the appropriate response. In a study of the aesthetic theories of Mill, Carlyle, Ruskin, and Arnold, Zelda Boyd demonstrates a concern in each writer with constructing a poetic theory which provides objective grounds for emotion. In referring to the same passage from Mill that I quoted above, Boyd argues:

> When Mill suggested that descriptions of nature could be used as the embodied equivalents of feeling to produce an effect in the reader equal to the effect of the actual scene, he was pointing the way that poetic theory was to go in the mid-nineteenth century. What was implied, first of all, was a fixed connection between objects and feelings that could serve as the basis for a symbolic, depersonalized art. The poet, while dealing with objective entities—scenes, situations, etc.—need not forsake the connection between poetry and feeling. If the scene were well-chosen and convincingly displayed, the poet could count on touching a respondent chord in the reader. Second, reality is regarded as independently shaped and given, undetermined by the perceiving and organizing and interpreting intelligence. The poet's function is to associate "bits" of simulated reality according to the emotions they engender, not unlike a child stringing beads according to color.[30]

Such a poetic theory implies a conception of the poet not as a creative agent of the divine, as the Romantics believed, but as a seer, who, knowing the properties of objects, can select and combine them appropriately. Each of the major Victorian critics in some way tries to fix an appropriate relationship between feelings and objects which derives our emotional response from the qualities of things in themselves. Carlyle moves away from the Romantic foundations of his thought in his increasing emphasis on the poet's faculty for objective vision. He praises the seeing eye of the poet "that discloses the inner harmony of things; what Nature meant. . . . Something she did mean." The poet does not half perceive and half create; he sees the meaning that is there. The emblem of the poet's art is not the lamp but the mirror, and "no *twisted*, poor convex-concave mirror, reflecting all objects with its own convexities and concavities; a perfectly *level* mirror." Like the Lady of Shalott, the poet recreates what he sees reflected in his mirror. "Art is not Artifice"; it reveals the meaning implicit in objects themselves.[31]

Like Carlyle, Arnold implies that meaning is inherent in the subjects of art:

What are the eternal objects of poetry, among all nations and at all times? They are actions; human actions; possessing an inherent interest in themselves, and which are communicated in an interesting manner by the art of the poet. Vainly will the latter imagine that he has everything in his own power; that he can make an intrinsically inferior action equally delightful with a more excellent one by his treatment of it. He may indeed compel us to admire his skill, but his work will possess, within itself, an incurable defect.

The poet, then, in the first place, has to select an excellent action; and what actions are the most excellent? Those, certainly, which most powerfully appeal to the great primary human affections: to those elementary feelings which subsist permanently in the race, and which are independent of time. These feelings are permanent and the same; that which interests them is permanent and the same also.[32]

In this passage, Arnold assumes a fixed connection between the subjects of art and feelings. Appropriate actions contain implicit within them the capacity to evoke appropriate responses. The poet's task is to select and combine those actions properly.

Ruskin's definition of the pathetic fallacy offers yet another attempt to fix the appropriate relation of feelings to objects. After dismissing objective and subjective as "tiresome and absurd words," Ruskin asserts:

We may go on at our ease to examine the point in question,—namely, the difference between the ordinary, proper, and true appearances of things to us; and the extraordinary, or false appearances, when we are under the influence of emotion, or contemplative fancy; false appearances, I say, as being entirely unconnected with any real power or character in the object, and only imputed to it by us.

The pathetic fallacy arbitrarily attributes human emotions to objects with which they have no natural connection. Weaker poets, among whom Ruskin numbers Keats and Tennyson, allow the pathetic fallacy into their work and thus admit "certain expressions and modes of thought which are in some sort diseased or false." The great poet can separate purely personal emotion from appropriate responses to objects. He can "keep his eyes fixed firmly on the *pure fact,* out of which if any feeling comes to him or his reader, he knows it must be a true one."[33]

Although Ruskin feels that too scientific an attitude toward natural phenomena causes man to lose a sense of nature's sublimity and mystery,[34] he nonetheless feels that the painter should be a naturalist, who, knowing the properties of visible objects, can select and combine them in his work. Ruskin devotes much of *Modern Painters* to minute description of the appearances of nature—leaves, branches, rocks, clouds—in order to provide a painter's dictionary of natural forms. Yet the catalogues of natural description in *Modern Painters* seem yet another example of the misplaced naturalism that characterizes Victorian literature, like the charts of isothermals and isobars which Tennyson kept in his room to insure the accuracy of his scientific allusions, because Ruskin, like Tennyson, insists upon scientific accuracy to portray what first appears to be an unnaturalistic ideal. *Modern Painters,* of course, was written to defend Turner. It seems as bizarre to defend Turner on realist grounds as to worry about the botanical specification in Tennyson's monologues, and it is important to understand Ruskin's conception of realism. Conventional painting, according to Ruskin, fosters the illusion that we see all objects clearly. We do not, Ruskin argues:

> Nature would have let you see, nay, would have compelled you to see, thousands of spots and lines, not one to be absolutely understood or accounted for, but yet all characteristic and different from each other; breaking light on shattered stones, vague shadows from waving vegetation, irregular stains of time and weather, mouldering hollows, sparkling casements—all would have been there—none, indeed, seen as such, none comprehensible or like themselves, but all visible; little shadows, and sparkles, and scratches, making that whole space of colour a transparent, palpitating, various infinity.[35]

It is this truth—a truth of visual impression—that Turner represents, but Ruskin is careful to attribute that truth not to the organizing intelligence of the viewer but to the organizing force of nature. Turner shows us just so much and no more "as nature would have allowed us to feel and see."[36]

In a way that paradoxically unites him to the French impressionists, Ruskin thus understands the realistic portrayal of nature to be an objective study of appearance, a "science of *Aspects*."[37] Ruskin felt, of course, that such study of appearances revealed the structure of the object and ultimately God's design of the universe. Nonetheless, Ruskin's stress upon impressions reveals how his extreme objectivism has an unlikely resemblance to a subjectivism he maintains as its diametrical opposite. Impressionism is so paradoxical a term in the history of both art and literature because it can assimilate both an extreme naturalism like Ruskin's and an extreme subjectivism like Pater's without mediating between the two. It strives to locate itself at the very juncture where, in Pound's words, "a thing outward and objective transforms itself or darts into a thing inward and subjective."[38] Pound's verbs suggest the ambiguity of the process. "Transforms itself" suggests a change in structure or composition; "darts into" can suggest merely a change in location. Victorian poetic theory for the most part maintains the second of Pound's definitions; good art portrays, in Ruskin's words, "the ordinary, proper, and true appearances of things to us." Victorian poetry, however, maintains Pound's ambiguity; it combines naturalistic fidelity to detail with absorption of objects into the medium of predominant emotion. It resolves the tension between subjective and objective appearances not by the dogmatic separation of proper from improper responses that we often find in the criticism but by leaving ambiguous its organizing principle.

Nowhere is the conflict between objective and subjective uses of the natural symbol more pronounced than in Pre-Raphaelitism. Pre-Raphaelitism has always been a problematic term in the history of Victorian poetry and painting because it seems to encompass such contradictory elements—fidelity to microscopic detail, the natural symbol, dreamlike poetry of vague reverie, absorption of objects to pattern and design. In the words of one critic, the Pre-Raphaelites were "curiously willing dualists."[39] They passed from an extreme naturalism to an abstract poetry of trance and dream with little sense of incongruity. They could do so because of the same concern with sensation that characterizes Tennyson and Ruskin. Ruskin, in fact, argued that Turner and the Pre-Raphaelite painters composed a single school of painting; that Turner was "the first and greatest of the Pre-

Raphaelites."[40] Ruskin can place the two in the same school for much the same reason that the Pre-Raphaelites themselves can so readily combine realistic detail with spiritual phantasmagoria. The artist's accurate rendering of impressions, whether those impressions are vague or distinct, automatically conveys the meaning implicit in phenomena.

Much Pre-Raphaelite painting holds the ideal of the self-sufficient natural symbol. Objects painted accurately enough declare their meaning. But our response to Pre-Raphaelite pictures suggests that natural objects do not declare their meaning in the way that the painters hoped that they might. On the one hand, objects often fail to declare their significance as plainly as the painter intended. We need Holman Hunt's title to tell us that his lovely portrait of grazing sheep are indeed "Strayed Sheep." On the other hand, the exaggerated naturalism of Pre-Raphaelite painting often succeeds not in conveying the symbolic significance of every object but in suggesting a morbid intensity of preoccupation. The extreme fidelity to minute detail in works like Hunt's "The Scapegoat" or Millais's "Ophelia" makes the paintings seem unnaturalistic, even expressionistic, in their depiction of their subjects.

Pre-Raphaelite poetry makes no attempt to portray natural symbols. Objects have a blank otherness as mere phenomena. In Rossetti's "The Woodspurge," for example, the woodspurge resists any meaning beyond its existence as a physical fact. The speaker of the poem wanders and then sits:

> Between my knees my forehead was,—
> My lips, drawn in, said not, Alas!
> My hair was over in the grass,
> My naked ears heard the day pass.
>
> My eyes, wide open, had the run
> Of some ten weeds to fix upon;
> Among those few, out of the sun,
> The woodspurge flowered, three cups in one.
>
> From perfect grief there need not be
> Wisdom or even memory:
> One thing then learnt remains to me,—
> The woodspurge has a cup of three.

The poem gives no meaning to the landscape beyond its mere existence. It introduces the possibility of a religious interpreta-

tion in "three cups in one" only to refuse the significance offered. Rossettti, as if following Ruskin's instruction to see only
what is there, goes to nature and finds only botanical specification. Like Ruskin, the speaker finds an anchor amid overpowering emotion in the accurate specification of natural fact, but the
poem refuses symbolic interpretation of that fact. In its purely
phenomenal existence, however, the landscape composes an impression which enables us to reconstruct the speaker's state of
mind. This state of mind offers little more possibility of interpretation—wisdom or memory—than the woodspurge. One
can only reexperience it by recombining its elements.

At first glance, Rossetti's poem seems to present a treatment
of objects very different from that of the painters' in their search
for the natural symbol, but the two methods are closely related.
An objective science of aspects, in which the perceiver's impressions realize the meaning within objects, can easily transform
itself to a subjective impressionism. The Pre-Raphaelites' attempt to create an art in which objects declare their own meaning thus can develop into an impressionism whose implicit
center is the psychology of the perceiver. Tennyson understood
this possibility and tried to evolve strategies to avoid it. The Pre-
Raphaelites were happy with the vaguely centered phantasmagoria to which their search for the natural symbol had led them.
Although Morris and Swinburne experiment with personae to
give center and resonance to perception in their poems, their
experiments are not motivated by the same desire for distance
and control as Tennyson's were.

Not all Victorian poetry manifests the tension I have been describing between a subjective impressionism and a science of aspects, and it is instructive to consider how poets who do not show
the tension manage the problem. Browning avoids the problem
through the strategy Tennyson also develops—the dramatic
monologue. Organizing a poem by the consciousness of a dramatic character makes objects take their meaning from the consciousness of that character. Arnold stops writing poetry in part
because objects fail to yield the meaning he desires. The self is
the only organizing principle that remains, and Arnold distrusts
the self as sufficient ground for poetry, so he turns to a critical
effort "to see the object as in itself it really is."

Hopkins is the only Victorian poet who resolves the tension
between the meaning objects have in themselves and our im-

pressions of them. An early poem from his notebook suggests
that the tension concerned him:

> It was a hard thing to undo this knot.
> The rainbow shines, but only in the thought
> Of him that looks. Yet not in that alone,
> For who makes rainbows by invention?
> And many standing round a waterfall
> See one bow each, yet not the same to all,
> But each a hand's breadth further than the next.
> The sun on falling waters writes the text
> Which yet is in the eye or in the thought.
> It was a hard thing to undo this knot.[41]

Hopkins here wishes some assurance that particular sense impressions have an identity with their generating object. The
poem asserts that Hopkins has solved the problem: "It *was* a
hard thing to undo this knot." This particular poem does not
explain how he undid it, but his later poetry repeatedly dramatizes his solution, which he names "instress." Hopkins gives instress two distinct meanings. At times he identifies instress with
the distinctiveness of an object; elsewhere he uses instress to
mean the perceiver's apprehension of the particular identity of
an object. By locating instress both in the object and in the viewer's perception of the object, Hopkins undoes the knot of his
early poem. His formulation of instress resembles Pound's description of the image, "when a thing outward and objective
transforms itself, or darts into a thing inward and subjective,"[42]
but Hopkins bases the identity he creates between object and
apprehension upon his conception of God. In the creation of the
universe, God charges it with a rhyming capacity which enables
man's imagination, his capacity of instress, to realize the divinely
ordained instress of the world. Hopkins conceives of the instress
man realizes as an active charge, a responsibility and a dynamic
address to the universe before him. He writes in *The Wreck of the
Deutschland:*

> I kiss my hand
> To the stars, lovely-asunder
> Starlight, wafting him out of it; and
> Glow, glory in thunder;
> Kiss my hand to the dappled-with-damson west:

Since, tho' he is under the world's splendour and wonder,
     His mystery must be instressed, stressed;
For I greet him the days I meet him, and bless when I
     understand.

In his emphasis on the active role the imagination plays in perception, Hopkins resembles the Romantics more closely than
any other major Victorian poet. But he nonetheless wishes to
maintain the identity of the thing perceived with his perception
of it in a way that allies him with Victorian poetics. Like Tennyson, he frequently seeks to use the representational power which
he imagines in sound to portray the essence of a thing. Language's chime and rhyme ideally manifest the chime and rhyme
of divine creation. By miming the shape of instress, the poet can
recreate that moment when impression realizes its object. But
Hopkins feared that language might manifest man's fallen, not
his divine, nature, that in its separateness from its object it might
reveal only man's self-taste, not the intricate design of the universe.[43] The "terrible sonnets" portray a world in which the
rhymes of man's speech torture him with the obsessive self-re-
flection that marks his distance from God: "this tormented mind
/ With this tormented mind tormenting yet." Thus even
Hopkins, who resolves the tension between subject and object
more successfully than other Victorian poets, is vulnerable to the
fear of solipsism.

Although Hopkins and Pater share a number of aesthetic attitudes, Pater lacks not only the theology that characterizes
Hopkins's poetry but also the theory of the imagination. Pater's
work contains the most extreme example in Victorian criticism of
a tension between a subjective impressionism and a science of
aspect. Experience for Pater is composed of momentary impressions. He talks much of the time as if these impressions were
idiosyncratic, private, incommunicable, "each mind keeping as a
solitary prisoner its own dream of a world." But at times Pater
speaks as if impressions were constituted of a number of elements
which the critic can disengage, much as a chemist can separate the
elements of a chemical compound, and thus reconstruct a formula for what has been a unique and momentary experience. In
the Preface to *The Renaissance*, Pater begins his definition of the
critic's task with Arnold's dictum:

"To see the object as in itself it really is," has been justly said to be the aim of all true criticism whatever; and in aesthetic criticism the first step towards seeing one's object as it really is, is to know one's own impression as it really is, to discriminate it, to realise it distinctly. The objects with which aesthetic criticism deals—music, poetry, artistic and accomplished forms of human life—are indeed receptacles of so many powers or forces: they possess, like the products of nature, so many virtues or qualities. What is this song or picture, this engaging personality presented in life or in a book, to *me*? What effect does it really produce on me? Does it give me pleasure? and if so, what sort or degree of pleasure? How is my nature modified by its presence, and under its influence? The answers to these questions are the original facts with which the aesthetic critic has to do; and, as in the study of light, of morals, of number, one must realise such primary data for oneself, or not at all.[44]

"*The* object" which Arnold desires to see becomes "one's object" for Pater; the formulation implies that there may be as many rainbows as there are people who look. The paragraph seems to transform Arnold's objectivism to an extreme subjectivism, whereby the critic cannot speak of the object as it really is but only of his personal impression: "One must realise such primary data for oneself, or not at all." Yet it soon becomes clear that Pater's impressions are produced not by an informing imagination or by the particular personality of the critic, but by a unique intersection of forces which affect a sensitive but passive perceiver. This perceiver can discriminate a false from a true impression: "what effect does it *really* produce on me?" In the next paragraph, Pater approaches even more closely a Ruskinian science of aspect:

The aesthetic critic, then, regards all the objects with which he has to do, all works of art, and the fairer forms of nature and human life, as power or forces producing pleasurable sensations, each of a more or less peculiar or unique kind. This influence he feels, and wishes to explain, by analyzing and reducing it to its elements. To him, the picture, the landscape, the engaging personality in life or in a book, *La Gioconda*, the hills of Carrara, Pico of Mirandola, are valuable for their virtues, as we say, in speaking of a herb, a wine, a gem; for the property each has of affecting one with a special, a unique, impression of pleasure. Our education becomes complete in proportion as our susceptibility to these impressions increases in depth and variety. And the function of the aesthetic critic is to distinguish, to analyze, and separate from its adjuncts, the virtue by which a picture, a landscape, a fair personality in life or in a book, produces this special impression of beauty or pleasure, to indicate what the source of that impression is, and under what conditions it is experienced. His end is reached when he has disengaged that virtue, and noted it, as a chemist notes some natural element, for himself and others.[45]

Although impressions are unique, they result from a combination of elements and conditions which can be disengaged and noted, thus analyzed as a chemist might analyze a compound and produce its formula. Such aesthetic formulae the critic notes "for himself and others." In his essays on individual artists, Pater always writes as if the impressions he describes are the impressions of any sensitive perceiver. He asks, for example, in his essay on Botticelli, "What is the peculiar sensation, what is the peculiar quality of pleasure, which his work has the property of exciting in us, and which we cannot get elsewhere?"[46]

Pater's critical goal of experiencing and analyzing the particular impression leads him to emphasize not the imagination with its forming capacity but the sensibility. A critic must have "a certain kind of temperament, the power of being deeply moved by the presence of beautiful objects."[47] Like Pater's conception of impressionism, his emphasis on sensibility allows without mediation an extreme subjectivism and a pronounced sensitivity to what is really there. As Yeats wrote in a criticism of Pater, "The soul becomes a mirror, not a brazier."[48] The question is only whether the mirror, in Carlyle's words, is "level or convex-concave."

In many ways Pater embodies the heritage of Victorian poetry and poses the problems that modern poetry seeks to solve. He refines experience to a number of fugitive impressions upon the acute sensibility, while he holds forth the dream that these impressions could contain within themselves objectivity and universal resonance without intervening discourse. Yeats, Eliot, and Pound all take that tension as the starting point of their poetics. The various ways in which they seek to resolve it determine the shape of modern poetry.

The three Victorian figures with whom Yeats most often associates his early poetry are Hallam, Rossetti, and Pater. He asserts, "When I began to write I avowed for my principles those of Arthur Hallam in his essay on Tennyson."[49] In *The Tragic Generation,* he calls Rossetti the most powerful subconscious influence upon himself and his contemporaries, and Pater the figure to whom "we looked consciously for our philosophy."[50] Yeats associates each of these figures with a pure poetry of the image. He came to reject the principles of all three for the limitation upon art and life to which the ideal of pure poetry committed them. Understanding Yeats's admiration and criticism of each of these writers will reveal how he assimilated and transformed his Victorian heritage.

Yeats understood Hallam to be saying that poetry is composed of the impressions of the world on the senses of highly sensitive men. Keats and Shelley "wrote out of the impression made by the world upon their delicate senses."[51] Such poetry does not admit moral philosophizing or intellectual generalization. It presents the moment when the poet apprehends "beauty wandering on her way." Yeats develops Hallam's idea of a poetry of sensation into a theory of symbolism.

> All sounds, all colours, all forms, either because of their preordained energies or because of long association, evoke indefinable and yet precise emotions, or, as I prefer to think, call down among us certain disembodied powers, whose footsteps over our hearts we call emotions; and when sound, and colour, and form are in a musical relation, a beautiful relation to one another, they become, as it were, one sound, one colour, one form, and evoke an emotion that is made out of their distinct evocations and yet is one emotion.[52]

It is easy to see the relationship of this definition of symbol to French symbolism. The essay in which it occurs begins with a reference to Symons's *The Symbolist Movement in Literature.* But there is little present in this definition that could not also derive from Hallam. He, too, felt that poetry combined sound, color, and form, to evoke an indefinable yet precise emotion.

Where Yeats differs from Hallam is in his resolute opposition to any faith that poetry derives its magic from imitating the real appearances of nature. Yeats uses the word picturesque with a kind of scorn for word painting. In "Art and Ideas," he writes that he developed Hallam's principles "to the rejection of all detailed description."[53] Like Hallam, Yeats would like to locate a source for the meaning and power of the materials of poetry independent of man's consciousness of them. Yeats would prefer to think not that the poet evokes emotions but that he calls down among us "certain disembodied powers." But those powers are not derived from the real appearances of nature, as Hallam implies; they are spiritual powers which work through those appearances.

In part because of his hostility to description, Yeats did not associate Tennyson but Keats, Shelley, and Rossetti with Hallam's principles. Yeats always spoke of Tennyson very much as Hallam spoke of Wordsworth; he accused him of writing an impure poetry which admitted moral values that were not aesthetic values. He was fond of quoting Verlaine's remark about *In Memoriam,* "When he should have been broken-hearted, he had many reminiscences."[54] When Yeats praises Rossetti, however, it is for writing a poetry very similar to the one Hallam identifies with Tennyson. More than any other Victorian poet, Rossetti portrays the intense moment of aesthetic contemplation in which nothing extrinsic—wisdom or memory—interferes: "He listens to the cry of the flesh till it becomes proud and passes beyond the world where some immense desire that the intellect cannot understand mixes with the desire for a body's warmth and softness."[55]

Yeats associates the artistic ideal that Rossetti embodies with an ideal of conduct. The poets of the nineties whom Rossetti influenced wrote a form of lyric which Yeats argues in *The Tragic Generation* put an almost unbearable pressure upon men's private lives. In its drive toward a moment of aesthetic contemplation unrelated to public interest or daily and vulgar passion, it paradoxically both attracted overwrought, unstable men and prevented them from achieving the integration they needed. In trying to explain the personal tragedies of many of his contemporaries of the nineties, Yeats questions the philosophy of life which their aesthetic ideal involved, a philosophy Yeats associates with Pater:

> If Rossetti was a subconscious influence, and perhaps the most powerful of all, we looked consciously to Pater for our

philosophy. Three or four years ago I re-read *Marius the Epicurean,* expecting to find I cared for it no longer, but it still seemed to me, as I think it seemed to us all, the only great prose in modern English, and yet I began to wonder if it, or the attitude of mind of which it was the noblest expression, had not caused the disaster of my friends. It taught us to walk upon a rope, tightly stretched through serene air, and we were left to keep our feet upon a swaying rope in a storm.[56]

When Yeats speaks of Pater, he frequently praises his prose style, as he does in the passage I have just quoted. Yeats justifies beginning his edition of *The Oxford Book of Modern Verse* with Pater's description of the Mona Lisa because of the influence it had upon poetic rhythm. But Yeats also wonders whether Pater had a more profound and potentially destructive influence in valuing an attitude of mind that limited poetry's emotional and moral range. In striving for an aesthetic ideality detached from public interest or common passion, Pater's philosophy may not have provided a way of incorporating either the swaying rope of a chaotic and passionate experience or the surrounding storm.

In criticizing the aesthetic ideal which Pater articulates, Yeats addresses both its solipsism and its objectivism. Yeats complains that the kind of poetry he and his contemporaries at The Cheshire Cheese strove to write left them "alone amid the obscure impressions of the senses."[57] But it also made the soul "a mirror, not a brazier." In the Introduction to *The Oxford Book of Modern Verse*, Yeats revises his criticism of the Victorians in terms that suggest his criticism of Pater's impressionism. The trouble was not that the Victorians had admitted so much "scientific humanitarian preoccupation, psychological curiosity, rhetoric." Rather, the difficulty was that "man became passive before a mechanized nature."[58] Yeats understands that such a philosophy results in a poetic impressionism like the one which Hallam and Pater articulate and much Victorian poetry embodies. Yeats laments that this impressionism still characterizes much modern poetry:

> It has sometimes seemed of late years, though not in the poems I have selected for this book, as if the poet could at any moment write a poem by recording the fortuitous scene or thought, perhaps it might be enough to put into

some fashionable rhythm—"I am sitting in a chair, and there are three dead flies on a corner of the ceiling."[59]

Of course, none of the poets with whom I am dealing would write such a poem, but their dogmatic assertion of some objects' fitness for sensation over others suggests the problem to which an impressionist poetics without a theory of the imagination could lead. Yeats ultimately attributes what he sees as the failure of *The Cantos* to such a passive philosophy of mind in the face of the flux of experience and relates that failure ultimately to Pater's influence,[60] a point to which I will return.

Yeats feels that modern art needs a theory of the active and integrating imagination that encompasses the entire personality. In the essay "Discoveries," he describes his movement from a poetry that presents states of pure imagination to one that incorporates the personality as a whole. He describes his early desire to present "nothing but states of mind, lyrical moments, pure essences." Yeats records his discovery that that ideal involves a passivity and a falseness to self: "as I imagined the visions outside myself my imagination became full of decorative landscape and of still life. I thought of myself as something unmoving and silent living in the middle of my own mind and body."[61] Yeats then determines to write a poetry that expresses the whole man, "blood, imagination, intellect running together." But it will not abandon its desire for essences. If choice had to be made, Yeats prefers "Shelley's chapel of the morning star to Burns' beer house." But he has an ideal of an art that can bring the two together: "we should ascend out of common interests, the thoughts of the newspapers, of the market-place, of men of science, but only so far as we can carry the normal, passionate, reasoning self, the personality as a whole."[62] The ideal of an art that can integrate the entire man brings Yeats to prefer Morris to Rossetti, not because he was the greater poet of the two but because "he was among the greatest of those who prepare the last reconciliation when the cross shall blossom with roses."[63]

One might argue that Hallam too, like Eliot later, holds an ideal of the reintegrated personality, that a poetry of sensation strives to present that moment when emotion, feeling, and thought exist as a single complex. But Yeats felt, in direct opposition to his early principles and to Hallam's and Eliot's poetics, that the kind of totality he desired could be achieved by admitting the very kinds of intellectual and moral discourse that he had previously striven to avoid. Yeats wrote in a diary he kept in 1909:

> Hallam argued that poetry was the impression on the senses of certain very sensitive men. It was such with the pure artists, Keats and Shelley, but not so with the impure artists who, like Wordsworth, mixed up popular morality with their work. I now see that the literary element in painting, the moral element in poetry, are the means whereby the two arts are accepted into the social order and become a part of life and not things of the study and the exhibition. Supreme art is a traditional statement of certain heroic and religious truths, passed on from age to age, modified by individual genius, but never abandoned.[64]

In his *Autobiography,* Yeats remarks that "My very remorse helped to spoil my early poetry, giving it an element of sentimentality through my refusal to permit it any share of an intellect which I considered impure."[65] Yet, admitting the intellect to poetry can dilute its effect in the very way for which he criticizes the Victorians. Yeats keeps his own poetry from that dilution by creating a dramatic context within the poem which makes reflection an element of the entire personality he strives to present.[66] Unlike Hallam and unlike the early Eliot and the early Pound, he strives to achieve a poetry that can use discourse as well as present the beauty of the image.

Yeats's reaction against the principles of Hallam's essay also involves a change in his conception of the symbol. From the beginning, Yeats distinguishes himself from the poets of the nineties by his desire for a popular symbolic language:

> Yet all the while envious of the centuries before the Renaissance, before the coming of our intellectual class with its separate interests, I filled my imagination with the popular beliefs of Ireland, gathering them up among forgotten novelists in the British Museum or in Sligo cottages. I sought some symbolic language reaching far into the past and associated with familiar names and conspicuous hills that I might not be alone amid the obscure impressions of the senses.[67]

The aesthetic derived from Hallam, Yeats argues, deprives art of a communal symbolic power: "in our poems an absorption in fragmentary sensuous beauty or detachable ideas had deprived us of the power to mould vast material into a single image."[68] Yeats calls the power to mold a single image which can express the energy of the whole man and the whole culture "our more profound Pre-Raphaelitism."[69] In doing so, he asserts both a continuity and a difference in his conception of the symbol. The Victorian tradition from which Yeats derives had used impressions of landscape to evoke moments of aesthetic contemplation, but it shares a symbolist poetics only in the sense that it uses combinations of sense impressions to evoke an emotion not named whose reexperience is the occasion of the poem. It seeks some necessary connection between object and emotion, but that necessity springs from physiology, a conviction of the necessary response that appearance evokes from us. Although it seeks to evoke that moment when beauty transfixes the soul, it rests upon a materialist, realist base. Yeats seeks with increasing deliberation a mythic conception of symbol more akin to the Romantic than the Victorian tradition whereby certain images embody eternal archetypes.

The development of Yeats's poetry does not show a sudden shift from one conception of symbol to another. From his earliest work, as he himself asserts in the passage quoted above, he is interested in popular and mythic symbols. But the change in his commitment from a poetry of sensation to a poetry that seeks to engage the whole man with all the rhetorical resources the poet possesses involves a difference in the way in which he depicts symbolic objects in his poetry. Here, for example, is a poem from *The Wind Among the Reeds* (1899), "The Song of Wandering Aengus":

> I went out to the hazel wood,
> Because a fire was in my head,
> And cut and peeled a hazel wand,
> And hooked a berry to a thread;
> And when white moths were on the wing,
> And moth-like stars were flickering out,
> I dropped the berry in a stream
> And caught a little silver trout.
>
> When I had laid it on the floor

> I went to blow the fire aflame,
> But something rustled on the floor,
> And someone called me by my name:
> It had become a glimmering girl
> With apple blossom in her hair
> Who called me by my name and ran
> And faded through the brightening air.
>
> Though I am old with wandering
> Through hollow lands and hilly lands,
> I will find out where she has gone,
> And kiss her lips and take her hands;
> And walk among long dappled grass,
> And pluck till time and tides are done
> The silver apples of the moon,
> The golden apples of the sun.

Yeats depicts a subject in this poem that preoccupies him throughout his poetic career—the relationship of man to an imaginative realm. Aengus pursues an imaginative absorption that always glimmers before him as a possibility that he can never realize. Yeats presents this state of consciousness by combining a number of images of glimmering and escape—white moths, moth-like stars, a glimmering girl fading through brightening air. The sense of light brightening and fading creates a feeling of ambiguous imaginative presence which one cannot definitively locate either in the landscape or in Aengus. Is it the fire in his head that sheds a glimmering light over the landscape, or does Aengus glimpse the reflection from some other world, whose reality he pursues? Yeats depends almost entirely upon sense impressions to create the image Aengus perceives. Like "Mariana," the poem thus uses sense impressions to sustain an ambiguity in its location of emotion. Even in his early poems like "The Rose Upon the Road of Time" or "The Two Trees," which give images a more separate symbolic significance, Yeats tends to evoke the image through aesthetic sensory contemplation.

Yeats's later poetry depends less upon perceptual than conceptual paradoxes. Here is the image of the tree from "Vacillation":

> A tree there is that from its topmost bough
> Is half all glittering flame and half all green
> Abounding foliage moistened with the dew;

And half is half and yet is all the scene;
And half and half consume what they renew,
And he that Attis' image hangs between
That staring fury and the blind lush leaf
May know not what he knows but knows not grief.

The image that Yeats constructs here uses paradox in a way that defies the formation of a single sense impression: "And half is half and yet is all the scene." Yeats's early images tend to evoke a coherent sensual impression though one that often relies heavily upon synaesthesia; Yeats's later images often strive to transcend the senses through a paradoxical overlayering of conflicting images: "Before me floats an image, man or shade, / Shade more than man, more image that a shade" ("Byzantium"). They depend upon abstract generalization to build their meaning: he that hangs Attis's image "may know not what he knows but knows not grief." The images demand not that you sense them but that you conceive them. They present not the experience of a sensibility but an imaginative construction.

Despite the ways in which Yeats makes images depend upon imaginative construction, however, he wants to claim for them a validity and existence beyond the personal imagination. His prose works not only create a structure for his poetry but attempt to claim that validation. In his attempt to make those claims, Yeats seeks the objectivity that other modern poets do. But Yeats does not seek to provide that objectivity whole without the mediation of the ego. Rather, he dramatizes man's individual tragic search for it. He not only makes the image depend on imaginative construction but embeds it in a poem that uses reflection, moral generalization, reminiscence—the very impurities he had previously disclaimed. He justifies those impurities by a very different sense of what a poem does. It does not enrapture a special sensibility but persuades a common audience. His model for the poet's art changes from music to oratory:

> Walter Pater says music is the type of all the arts, but somebody else, I forget now who, that oratory is their type. You will side with the one or the other according to the nature of your energy, and I in my present mood am all for the man who, with an average audience before him, uses all means of persuasion—stories, laughter, tears, and but so much music as he can discover on the wings of words.[70]

Furthermore, Yeats strives to write a poetry that involves all of man's faculties. Reflection and reminiscence give Yeats access to a psychological and moral range that extends poetry's power. He incorporates these diverse modes through a theory of personality and imagination that unites image and discourse in a dramatic event.

Yeats resolves the problem of the image in much the same way that he resolves the problem of voice. He still seeks the objectivity that characterizes modern poetry, but he incorporates the objective realm of symbols, like the mask, into a lyric of multiple voice whose organizing principle is the imagination. In contrast to Yeats, Eliot and Pound never evolve such a theory of the imagination. Much like the Victorians, they strive to create a poetics that gives objective equivalents and validation to feeling.

Eliot's early poetry and criticism display a conflict between a conviction that experience is peculiar and private, "a circle closed on the outside . . . opaque to the others which surround it," and a desire for allegiance to some external authority. One of the ways that Eliot sought to resolve this conflict is by his conception of the objective correlative. The objective correlative bears striking similarities to Hallam's poetry of sensation; both rely upon sensation to resolve a tension between subject and object they would like to avoid.

Eliot feels that literature expresses personal emotion. He assumes in the essay on *Hamlet,* in which he defines the objective correlative, that the play expresses the emotion of some experience that Shakespeare had. Eliot wonders, although he admits that he can never know, "under compulsion of what experience [Shakespeare] attempted to express the inexpressibly horrible."[71] The poet expresses the emotion he chooses as the subject of his work by finding the appropriate objective correlative, "a set of objects, a situation, a chain of events which shall be the formula of that *particular* emotion; such that when the external facts, which must terminate in sensory experience, are given, the emotion is immediately evoked."[72] Despite Eliot's repeatedly expressed distaste for Pater, his account of aesthetic experience is remarkably similar to Pater's. Literature composes unique formulas for experience which affect a sensitive but passive perceiver in a determined way. Eliot, like Pater, achieves a universality for private experience by depending upon sensation as the experience art offers. Objects implictly contain the power of evoking particular sensations. The artist combines these objects in such a way as to create the adequate counter or objective correlative for his emotion. Like Ruskin, like Hallam, Eliot uses sensation to make emotion a quality inevitably evoked by certain objects. He thus avoids the solipsism that he fears as a condition of consciousness. As he writes in his essay on Dante, "Speech varies, but our eyes are all the same."[73]

Eliot's attempt to make emotion necessarily consequent to our sensations of objects leads to an emphasis, like that in Victorian criticism, upon right vision: "the first condition of right thought is right sensation."[74] Eliot often recalls Ruskin and Arnold in his praise for seeing the object as it really is without any interfering ego. In explaining the superiority of Lancelot Andrewes's sermons to those of Donne, Eliot writes:

> Andrewes's emotion is purely contemplative; it is not personal, it is wholly evoked by the object of contemplation, to which it is adequate; his emotions wholly contained in and explained by its object. But with Donne there is always the something else. . . . Donne is a "personality" in a sense in which Andrewes is not; his sermons, one feels, are a "means of self-expression." He is constantly finding an object which shall be adequate to his feelings; Andrewes is wholly absorbed in the object and therefore responds with the adequate emotion.[75]

Like Ruskin and Arnold, Eliot feels that the object itself provokes adequate emotion if one can only free oneself of interfering personality. In the view of Donne's sermons expressed in this essay, Eliot criticizes Donne for not being able to see the object as it is. Eliot's earlier view of Donne is of course quite different, but the terms in which he establishes his judgment are precisely similar. In an earlier essay, Eliot praises Donne for seeing the object as it is. He uses as an example the image of bright hair about the bone from "The Relic."

> A poet of morbidly keen sensibilities but weak will might become absorbed in the hair to the exclusion of the original association which made it significant. A poet of imaginative or reflective power more than emotional power would endow the hair with ghostly or moralistic meaning. Donne sees the thing as it is.[76]

Eliot's description of Donne's excellence here has a remarkable resemblance to Ruskin's definition of the pathetic fallacy. The lesser poet allows his personal sensibilities or ideas to interfere with his vision. The great poet can keep his eyes firmly on the pure fact, can see the thing as it is, and so write a poetry whose images generate appropriate emotion.

Eliot's attempt to generate emotion by the qualities of objects leads him to praise clear visual images. He praises Dante's "visual imagination,"[77] for example, and one has the sense that he would like to assimilate the spiritual to the physical meaning of the term. If we see what Dante saw, we might in fact see his visions. Eliot depends upon a similar ambiguity in asserting that poetic drama deals with "emotions such as observation can confirm."[78] Particularly in his early criticism, Eliot seeks to make physical observation imply observations of judgment and value.

Eliot's emphasis upon sensation sometimes leads him to treat the poet's power as a matter of physiological organization. In his essay on Massinger, he argues that Massinger's relative inferiority as a dramatist resulted from an undeveloped physiological organization: "The tragedy of Massinger is interesting chiefly according to the definition given before; the highest degree of verbal excellence compatible with the most rudimentary development of the senses."[79] Eliot again recalls Pater in his emphasis upon the physical refinement of sensibility: "Had Massinger had a nervous system as refined as that of Middleton, Tourneur, Webster, or Ford, his style would be a triumph."[80]

Much as Eliot occasionally treats style as a consequence of physiological refinement, he sometimes speaks as if words could compose a neutral medium for the sensation of objects. He praises the poets he admires for a transparency of language to sensation. In the metaphysical period, "the intellect was immediately at the tips of the senses. Sensation became word and word was sensation."[81] He criticizes Swinburne for creating a world exclusively of words. "Language in a healthy state presents the object, is so close to the object that the two are identified."[82] Literature progresses through its attempt "to digest and express new objects, new groups of objects, new feelings, new aspects, as, for instance, the prose of Mr. James Joyce or the earlier Conrad."[83] One might object to the application of such a definition to the work of Joyce or Conrad or of Eliot himself, all of whom like Donne explore the ways in which the conditions of syntax

affect perception. But despite the more complicated understanding of the relationship of sensation, emotion, and language
that Eliot's poetry reflects, his criticism often strives to make
emotion an automatic consequence of sensation.

Some critics have treated the objectivism of Eliot's criticism as
a brilliant rhetorical maneuver through which he obscures the
subversive and Modernist elements of his poetry.[84] Whatever
the rhetorical advantages his criticism provided him, however,
Eliot's classicism has a complex relationship to the poetic theory
of the previous century. Few readers of Eliot now deny his connection as a poet and as a critic with the Romanticism from
which he tried to dissociate himself,[85] but the way in which Eliot
seeks to transform Romanticism has a less frequently recognized
but important kinship to Victorian poetic theory. Eliot shares
with the Romantics an idealist epistemology but fears the subjectivism that he feels is implicit within it. He seeks to avoid that
subjectivism through a theory of the poetic image that emphasizes right sensation. The poet can communicate emotional experience through finding the sensory formula for the emotion
he wishes to convey. There is of course an important difference
between such formulas and Victorian poetic images. The Victorian seeks the subject from which he derives the appropriate
emotional response; Eliot seeks appropriate equations between
emotions and synthetic combinations of images. Nonetheless,
Eliot resembles the Victorians in using sensation to objectify personal emotion. The objective correlative thus provides a strategy
like that of the dramatic monologue. It recognizes the inescapable subjectivity of experience while it enables the poet to claim
objectivity in his representation of that experience.

In order to construct such a poetics, Eliot must assume that
analysis of sensation, carried on with the requisite detachment
and acuity, will automatically produce principle and definition.
In "The Perfect Critic," Eliot argues that Aristotle's excellence
consists in the disinterested analysis of sensation. Eliot begins his
argument by dismissing the man of ordinary intelligence who
might

> like one poet because he reminds him of himself, or an-
> other because he expresses emotions which he admires; he
> may use art, in fact, as the outlet for the egotism which is
> suppressed in his own specialty. But Aristotle had none of

these impure desires to satisfy; in whatever sphere of interest, he looked solely and steadfastly at the object; in his short and broken treatise he provides an eternal example—not of laws, or even of method, for there is no method except to be very intelligent, but of intelligence itself swiftly operating the analysis of sensation to the point of principle and definition.[86]

Eliot would like to believe that facts "generalize themselves."[87] He speaks of impressions and perceptions as if they had an inherent structure which automatically realizes itself in the disinterested sensitive mind: "the perceptions do not, in a really appreciative mind, accumulate as a mass, but form themselves as a structure; and criticism is the statement in language of this structure; it is a development of sensibility."[88] Eliot criticizes the Romantics because they would make the individual imagination the agent of that structure. In "The Function of Criticism," Eliot criticizes Goethe and Coleridge for letting their imaginations color fact: "The real corrupters are those who supply opinion or fancy; and Goethe and Coleridge are not guiltless—for what is Coleridge's *Hamlet:* is it an honest inquiry as far as the data permit, or is it an attempt to present Coleridge in an attractive costume?"[89] *Hamlet* is for Eliot the example of the incompletely realized work of art for the very reason that it is so central to Romantic criticism; the emotion in excess of the facts as they appear which Eliot so much distrusts is the very testimony to the imagination's power that the Romantics exalt. Eliot would like to clarify and reduce those nebulous emotions "to a state of fact."[90]

Eliot's criticism often reveals his awareness of the complex philosophical issues that his poetics at once imply and scant. "The Function of Criticism," Eliot's most dogmatic insistence upon the adequacy of fact to imply interpretation, ends with the following statement: "But if anyone complains that I have not defined truth, or fact, or reality, I can only say apologetically that it was no part of my purpose to do so, but only to find a scheme into which, whatever they are, they will fit, if they exist."[91] Eliot's poetry offers a similar skeptical background against which to place the objectivism of his criticism. Like this statement, it seems to offer possibilities of indeterminacy precisely the opposite of the goal his poetics implies. In an even more pronounced way than Tennyson, Eliot attempts to make sensation the sufficient carrier of meaning. He paradoxically creates a poetry whose organizing principle is often so ambiguous that it frees words and images to become not objective correlatives but indefinite emotions for which the reader has remarkable license "to find a scheme into which, whatever they are, they will fit, if they exist."

As Eliot's theory of the objective correlative implies, his early poetry uses combinations of sense impressions without the interpretation of discursive statement to evoke states of consciousness. Here, for example, is the first section of "Preludes":

> The winter evening settles down
> With smell of steaks in passageways.
> Six o'clock.
> The burnt-out ends of smoky days.
> And now a gusty shower wraps
> The grimy scraps
> Of withered leaves about your feet
> And newspapers from vacant lots.
> The showers beat
> On broken blinds and chimney pots,
> And at the corner of the street
> A lonely cab-horse steams and stamps.
> And then the lighting of the lamps.

Eliot's use of landscape here resembles Tennyson's in "Mariana." Eliot combines very particular objective details—the smell of steaks, broken blinds, chimney pots—with anthropomorphic details that suggest a human perceiver—the lonely cab-horse, the burnt-out ends of smoky days. Yet the passage presents only the landscape as acting—the evening settles, the shower wraps, the horse steams and stamps. The poem creates an ambiguity in its location of emotion similar to that in "Mariana." Does the landscape automatically produce the emotional effect implied? Or do we know the perceiving consciousness through the environment it creates? Eliot, like Tennyson, seeks the identity of the two. The poem gives "the thousand sordid images of which your soul is constituted," but it also implies that those images contain in themselves the potential to evoke the emotion which is the poem's subject. Sensory experience thus enables Eliot to write a poetry which can objectify those peculiar and private experiences which constitute consciousness. The fusion of emotion with landscape becomes so complete that by the end of the poem it is difficult to tell whether the poem concerns the soul of some imagined city-dweller or the city itself.

> His soul stretched tight across the skies
> That fade behind a city block
> Or trampled by insistent feet
> At four and five and six o'clock;
> And short square fingers stuffing pipes,
> And evening newspapers, and eyes
> Assured of certain certainties,
> The conscience of a blackened street
> Impatient to assume the world.

Although the differences in imagery, tone, style, and rhythm make "Preludes" seem very distant from Tennyson's "Claribel." the two poems use the identity of consciousness and landscape to similar purpose. The ambiguity in the poems' subjects allows both poets to make a state of consciousness implicit in the objects of its focus. The landscape at one and the same time expresses and objectifies personality.

Eliot, of course, writes a poetry different from Victorian poetry in many important respects. He eliminates the narrative dimension that locates most Victorian poems at a particular time and place. We often have a story in Tennyson that situates the moment of lyric emotion, whereas the plots of Eliot's poems are most often ambiguous. Tennyson imagines a scene that contains the objects through which he evokes a state of consciousness; Eliot brings together objects to compose a synthetic interior landscape, as in this passage from "Gerontion":[92]

> My house is a decayed house,
> And the jew squats on the window sill, the owner,
> Spawned in some estaminet of Antwerp,
> Blistered in Brussels, patched and peeled in London.
> The goat coughs in the field overhead;
> Rocks, moss, stonecrop, iron, merds.
> The woman keeps the kitchen, makes tea,
> Sneezes at evening, poking the peevish gutter.

In this passage, Eliot does not locate the house Gerontion inhabits in a single place, but seeks to suggest through it all the decaying houses of Europe. Furthermore, he identifies house and owner so that the house reflects the characteristics of its landlord, "Spawned in some estaminet of Antwerp, / Blistered in Brussels, patched and peeled in London." The parallel structure of these two lines seems to make the participles modify "owner," but houses are more often than people blistered, patched, and peeled. The adjectives seem at once to characterize owner, window sill, house, even Gerontion. Eliot thus extends the landscape of his poem at the same time that he increases the poem's ambiguity. He uses images—"Rocks, moss, stonecrop, iron, merds"—not to describe a scene but to evoke a set of associations. Furthermore, he uses a far wider range of tone than the Victorian landscape poem. All of these characteristics of Eliot's poetic style—the synthesizing of landscape, the reduction of narrative, the range of tone—make his poems discontinuous, ambiguous, difficult.

Eliot's omission of explanatory and connecting matter in the construction of landscape places great demands upon the reader to compose the landscapes of his poems. In the preface he wrote for Perse's *Anabase*, Eliot discusses the way in which the suppression of explanatory links affects the reading process. His discussion recalls Hallam's description of the reading process in his definition of the picturesque. Eliot first asserts that any obscurity in Perse's poem results from "the suppression of 'links in the chain,' or explanatory and connecting matter." He continues:

> The justification of such abbreviation of method is that the sequence of images coincides and concentrates into one intense impression of barbaric civilization. The reader has to allow the images to fall into his memory successively without questioning the reasonableness of each at the moment; so that, at the end, a total effect is produced.
>
> Such selection of a sequence of images and ideas has nothing chaotic about it. There is a logic of the imagination as well as a logic of concepts.[93]

Like Hallam, Eliot argues that poetic images contain within themselves a necessary logic which a reader of proper receptiveness will experience. Such a logic depends upon an implied law of association. Because cetain images evoke a certain effect, they may become the objective correlative of the poet's emotion without the need for interpreting discourse.

Like Tennyson, Eliot uses the dramatic monologue to provide a center which locates images within the radius of a perceiving consciousness. In the course of his poetic career, however, Eliot defines the perceiver in increasingly general terms. J. Alfred Prufrock and the speaker of "A Portrait of A Lady" are clearly individuated characters, but Gerontion is a type, and the figure of Tiresias unites all of the characters of *The Waste Land* in a single mythical presence. Eliot refers the perceptions which compose his poems to an increasingly generalized representation of man's consciousness. This development reflects the objectivist thrust of his poetics; yet, the less particularized the perceiving consciousness, the greater the possibilities for ambiguity. Eliot's poetry thus embodies a central paradox: it implies a universal meaning which the poetic facts determine while it admits an extraordinarily high degree of indeterminacy. The dream that objects without interpreting discourse can carry their own meaning not merely for a single consciousness but for the whole mind of Europe commits Eliot to a poetry that contains a far greater amount of ambiguity than more Romantically based theories of poetic composition do.

The tension between Eliot's poetics and his poetry raises the question of his attitude toward the indeterminacy his poetry contains. He in fact frequently asserts that a poem may appear to mean many different things to many different readers, that an author is just another reader of his own work. Yet this stance of Eliot's, far from implying a relativist attitude toward poetic meaning, involves the same distrust of discourse and of language as a medium with its own laws that his conception of the image implies. Our differing interpretations are all partial formulations, ghosts, of an essential meaning which the poem intimates. Eliot writes in "The Music of Poetry":

> the poet is occupied with frontiers of consciousness beyond which words fail, though meanings still exist. A poem may appear to mean very different things to different readers, and all of these meanings may be different from what the author thought he meant. . . . The reader's interpretation may differ from the author's and be equally valid—it may even be better. . . . The different interpretations may all be partial formulations of one thing; the ambiguities may be due to the fact that the poem means more, not less, than ordinary speech can communicate.[94]

Like Tennyson, Eliot feels that the music of poetry carries this essential meaning. He therefore exploits music and the impression of words, much as Tennyson does, to make music a sign where words fail. He writes in "Burnt Norton":

> Words strain
> Crack and sometimes break, under the burden,
> Under the tension, slip, slide, perish,
> Decay with imprecision, will not stay in place,
> Will not stay still
>
> . . . .
>
>   Only by the form, the pattern
> Can words or music reach
> The stillness.

A number of modern theories of poetic language would deny the possibility of that essentialist meaning for which Eliot's poetry and poetics strive. Eliot feared that this might be the case, as the first passage I quoted from "Burnt Norton" implies. In "The Perfect Critic," Eliot laments the tendency of words to become "indefinite emotions."[95] Yet in many ways his poetry brilliantly exploits that possibility just as it brilliantly depicts the subjectivism Eliot strove to escape. When Eliot's poetry is at its best, it expresses the tragic chasm between what words do not mean and what we would have them mean, between man's imprisonment in his own consciousness and his desire to participate in a community in which value is given from the outside. Much like the Victorian poetry and poetics, Eliot's poetry and poetics express two responses to a central problem. His prose attempts to assert objective validation for images; his poetry explores the ambiguity of the organizing principle which his poetics involves.

Much like Tennyson's poetic career, Eliot's career suggests how fragile is the enterprise to which his own poetics have committed him. Like Tennyson, like Yeats, he ultimately admits a discursive voice into his poetry. The *Four Quartets*, like *In Memoriam*, frequently use abstract theological discourse to convey its meaning. The dogmatism into which the *Quartets* occasionally fall again suggests the difficulty Eliot had in making images themselves convey a meaning he wanted to believe was implicit within them. And his turning to the drama, like Tennyson's turning to narrative poetry, implies an abandonment of his earlier imagistic enterprise.

Unlike Eliot and unlike Yeats, Pound does not alter his demand that the image convey its own significance. *The Cantos* demand perhaps more radically than any poem in English that images imply their own meaning. In his early criticism, Pound talks about the image as an alternative to the persona. In his essay in which he defines vorticism, he asserts that he began "the search for the real" by constructing masks. He continues:

> Secondly, I made poems like "The Return," which is an objective reality and has a complicated sort of significance, like Mr. Epstein's "Sun God," or Mr. Brzeska's "Boy with a Coney." Thirdly, I have written "Heather," which represents a state of consciousness, or "implies," or "implicates" it. . . .
>
> These two latter sorts of poem are impersonal, and that fact brings us back to what I said about absolute metaphor. They are Imagisme . . . .

As Pound develops his definition of imagism, he explains, "Browning's 'Sordello' is one of the finest *masks* ever presented. Dante's 'Paradiso' is the most wonderful *image*."[96] These two passages imply that the image and the mask serve similar functions for Pound; they both allow him to objectify emotion.

In his early criticism, Pound asserts that the writer should treat emotion as yet another object in a world of objects. The first tenet of the Imagiste faith, which he formulated in 1912, urges "direct treatment of the 'thing' whether subjective or objective."[97] In 1914, he praises Joyce in the following terms: "he deals with subjective things, but he presents them with such clarity of outline that he might be dealing with locomotives or with builders' specifications."[98] Like Ruskin, Pound objectifies emotions through a theory of impressionism. The same essay on Joyce from which I have just quoted proceeds to identify Joyce with the impressionists. Pound distinguishes two schools of impressionism: a school of prose and verse writers stemming from Stendhal and Flaubert who deal in "exact presentation," and a school of verse writers who emulate the softness of Monet's paintings. It is the first school, of course, that Pound himself emulates. Pound seeks to write a poetry that expresses the scientific, objective aspect of impressionism. In discussing "In a Station of the Metro," he expresses his intention in the following way: "In a poem of this sort one is trying to record the precise instant when a thing outward and objective transforms itself, or darts into a thing inward and subjective."[99] I have already suggested in discussing Pound's formulation in the context of the Victorian tradition that the statement contains an ambiguity in its verbs "transforms itself" and "darts into." Like the Victorians, Pound assumes that objects have within themselves the power to produce specific emotional resonances which the artist manipulates. He refers approvingly to Kandinsky's chapter "The Language of Form and Colour" in *Concerning the Spiritual in Art,* in which Kandinsky argues that color and form have specific internal resonances which the painter can manipulate to produce a purposive vibration in the human soul.[100] Pound makes a similar assumption about literature when he calls poetry "a sort of inspired mathematics, which gives us equations, not for abstract figures, triangles, spheres and the like, but equations for the human emotions."[101] In his essay on vorticism, he again defines the image in terms of the equation. He distinguishes four kinds of mathematical equations. The fourth and most "intense" kind, the equation of analytical geometry, defines universal recurrent form in the same way in which great art does so: "By the 'image' I mean such an equation; not an equation of mathematics, not something about *a, b,* and *c,* having to do with form, but about *sea, cliffs, night,* having something to do with mood."[102] Sea, cliffs, and night, or petals, wet, black, and bough have implicit within them the capacity to evoke specific emotions which the poet can manipulate through manipulating those objects. The way in which Pound uses a scientific vocabulary to define impressionism recalls Ruskin. Pound repeatedly asserts that this is not symbolism, which indeed it is not. The objects do not suggest an emotion or mood separable from them; they themselves contain it. Pound can therefore assert that the natural object is always the adequate symbol.[103] Much like Ruskin, he believes that objects inevitably evoke certain feelings. The writer who presents them exactly, who treats them directly, will therefore transfer their emotional energies to the reader. The enormous emphasis that Pound places upon technique results in part from his objectivism. Like Ruskin, he feels that the more accurate the representation, the more clearly the significance of the subject will declare itself.

On the basis of Pound's realism, Donald Davie has sharply distinguished between Pound's images and Eliot's objective correlatives. He asserts that for Pound

> One cardinal case of "the image" . . . is the carefully exact image the biologist constructs of the organisms he studies—an image created by nothing more recondite than scrupulously close and disciplined observation of the object as his senses apprehend it. It is not clear whether this is ever in T. S. Eliot's mind when he uses the word "image"; it is difficult to see how it can be, for "image" as Eliot used the word, seems to comprise also what he has called "the objective correlative." And according to Eliot, the artist, in constructing his objective correlative out of phenomena offered to his senses, is not at all interested in those phenomena for themselves, in their objectivity, but only to the extent that they may stand in for the subjective phenomena (such as states of mind or feeling) which can thus be objectified through them.[104]

It is true, as Davie argues, that Eliot frequently begins from an idealist position which he attempts to objectify, but Eliot implies at other times that one cannot separate a consciousness from the objects of its perception. Although Pound has a more consistently realist orientation than Eliot, he nonetheless often expresses a concern with objectifying mythic intuition. The doctrine of the image and the objective correlative allow Pound and Eliot, respectively, to identify inward and outward. Even when they start from opposite positions, and they do not always do so, they both seek to represent that instant when inner and outer meet. It is precisely the point central to the enterprise of impressionism that it can encompass both an idealist and a realist position because it seeks to assimilate idealism to realism.[105]

Like Ruskin, Pound conceives of impressionism as a dynamic ideal. He wants to evoke what Ruskin calls "a transparent palpitating various infinity." He moves from imagism to vorticism to accomodate his sense of the way in which poetry dynamically engages energy. Yet his emphasis on process and movement does not diminish his stress on objectivity. In the paragraph in which he defines vorticism, he concludes by quoting Aquinas's statement, "Nomina sunt consequentia rerum."[106]

As the quotation from Aquinas reflects, Pound adapts a theory of language to accommodate his conception of the image. He finds a theoretical structure to defend his identification of words and things in the work of Fenollosa. Pound embraces Fenollosa's theory for many of the same reasons that he chooses vorticism as a definition of his poetry. Like vorticism, Fenollosa's theory of the Chinese written character asserts a dynamic conception of the operations of language and art. But Fenollosa bases his dynamism upon an objective equation between words and the processes of nature. Language in a healthy state is a transparent medium for the transferences of force that constitute the operations of nature. Language is successive because the operations of nature are successive. Fenollosa uses the example of observing a man see a horse.

> In speech we split up the rapid continuity of this action and of its picture into its three essential parts or joints in the right order, and say:
>
> Man sees horse.
>
> It is clear that these three joints, or words, are only three phonetic symbols, which stand for the three terms of a natural process.[107]

Chinese is superior to other languages because it maintains the natural connection between thing and sign; Chinese notation "is based upon a vivid shorthand picture of the operations of nature." "In reading Chinese we do not seem to be juggling mental counters, but to be watching *things* work out their own fate."[108]

As the sentence that I have just quoted implies, Fenollosa's theory of language seeks to avoid the very subjective predication on which the Romantic conception of imagination is based. In a discussion of why the sentence form exists, Fenollosa dismisses the hypothesis that it unites a subject and a predicate because

> the grammarian falls back on pure subjectivity. *We* do it all; it is a little private juggling between our right and left hands. The subject is that about which *I* am going to talk; the predicate is that which *I* am going to say about it. The sentence according to this definition is not an attribute of nature but an accident of man as a conversational animal.
>
> If it were really so, then there could be no possible test of the truth of a sentence.

Fenollosa wants the sentence form implicit within the form of nature itself: "The sentence form was forced upon primitive man by nature itself. It was not we who made it; it was a reflection of the temporal order in causation."[109] Similarly, Fenollosa locates metaphor within nature herself: "But the primitive metaphors do not spring from arbitrary subjective processes. They are possible only because they follow objective lines of relations in nature herself."[110]

As Herbert Schneidau argues, Fenollosa's theory implies a boundless faith in the power of language to reflect objects.[111] It also contains a boundless Ruskinian faith in the capacity of objects to contain within themselves their own meaning. This faith in the transparency of language and the implicit meaning of objects allows Pound to think of passages and entire works of art as facts, data, specimens that generalize themselves, that imply necessary conclusions. Pound conceives of both artist and critic as scientists who see the law implicit in phenomena. The artist places the data in such a way that it implies the necessary conclusion to the reader. The critic, by seeking the object as it really is, by "the examination and juxtaposition of particular specimens" acquires and transmits knowledge.[112] "An idea is only an imperfect induction from fact."[113]

Pound's conception of art as the presentation of materials for an analysis implicit within them paradoxically commits him to a poetry, like Eliot's, that contains a very high degree of indeterminacy. The desire for an art in which images imply their own meaning leads him to eliminate a controlling "I" and moralizing discourse. Images, once set free, do not necessarily cohere in the way Pound had in mind. His poetry thus admits the very subjectivism and pluralism which his poetics seeks to eliminate.

The imagist poems which Pound wrote in 1913 and 1914 and which are collected in *Lustra* use sense impressions to implicate a state of consciousness. Here, for example, is "Heather":

> The black panther treads at my side,
> And above my fingers
> There float the petal-like flames.
>
> The milk-white girls
> Unbend from the holly - trees,
> And their snow-white leopard
> Watches to follow our trace.

Previously I quoted a passage in which Pound names this poem as an example of one of the stages of his "search for the real"; he claims that it is impersonal, an absolute metaphor, yet he explicitly dissociates the poem from symbolism. Like the title "In a Station of the Metro," the title "Heather" asserts a naturalist context for the vision. Pound wrote in a letter to his father, "The title is put on it to show that the poem is a simple statement of facts occurring to the speaker." But he continues, "these facts do not occur on the same plane with his feet, which are solidly planted in a climate producing Heather and not leopards."[114] Much like Mill or Hallam, Pound asserts that the poem is a response to the real appearances of nature. Yet without its title, the poem seems to work much like a symbolist poem in which words, set free from naturalistic or discursive context, imply sensory and mythic associations that evoke awareness of some ideal presence in consciousness. Pound's poem takes its peculiar power from the tension between the naturalistic context of its title and the symbolist evocation of its body. This tension makes ambiguous the poem's organizing principle. It locates itself at the moment when "a thing outward and objective transforms itself, or darts into a thing inward and subjective." Like Tennyson's and Eliot's use of landscape, Pound's poem sustains the ambiguity of that formulation.

A short poem like "Heather" carefully circumscribes that tension and ambiguity. Pound frequently used this imagistic method of compostion in longer poems which do not circumscribe the ambiguity so narrowly. The "Medallion" that closes *Hugh Selwyn Mauberley* is an example. The poem presents a carefully wrought image inspired by the appearance of a woman singing:

> Luini in porcelain!
> The grand piano
> Utters a profane
> Protest with her clear soprano.
>
> The sleek head emerges
> From the gold-yellow frock
> As Anadyomene in the opening
> Pages of Reinach.
>
> Honey-red, closing the face-oval,
> A basket-work of braids which seem as if they were
> Spun in King Minos' hall
> From metal, or intractable amber;

The face-oval beneath the glaze,
Bright in its suave bounding-line, as,
Beneath half-watt rays,
The eyes turn topaz.

"Medallion" resembles many of Pound's early poems; it uses images to depict a moment of aesthetic awareness. Yet this moment is not given the kind of emphasis and value which isolation within an independent piece gives Pound's earlier images. Rather, it is set within the very complex context of *Mauberley*, which nonetheless gives no direct indication of how we are to read this poem. The images themselves thus carry an enormous burden of meaning, while the entire poem allows them a considerable degree of indeterminacy. Critics debate whose poem it is, what it means, what statement its tone implies. The very fact of the debate suggests the difficulties Pound's method imposes. The images intimate some undeclared central perception from which they emanate, but the reader must construct that center for himself. The burden of meaning that Pound places upon the image thus commits him to a poetry that allows the very relativism and subjectivism that his poetics seems designed to combat.

Nowhere is this paradox more evident than in *The Cantos*, where Pound attempts to write an epic poem out of lyric materials in which there is no controlling voice. The extraordinary difficulties which *The Cantos* presents result from Pound's ambition to write a poem in which images declare their own meaning. The obscurity and fragmentation of *The Cantos*, its layering of civilizations, make it seem very distant from Victorian aesthetics. Yet its motivating epistemology—that seeing the object as it really is, without the interfering and falsifying ego, reveals a structure implicit in the order of things—develops directly from Victorian poetics. And like the Victorians, Pound relies upon a didactic commentary at many points in the poem in order to make it all cohere, as if the welter of particulars he has juxtaposed generated some compensatory need for overdetermination. It is a profound irony that a poetics so bent on seeing an order manifest in things should ultimately motivate both a return to the didacticism from which it had initially rebelled and a poetry of such indeterminacy.

In his Introduction to *The Oxford Book of Modern Verse*, Yeats explicitly relates the philosophy of *The Cantos* to Pater. "Did Pater foreshadow a poetry, a philosophy, where the individual is nothing, the flux of *The Cantos* of Ezra Pound?"[115] Yeats's question implies a complex historical relationship. Pater presages a sense shared by Yeats, Pound, and Eliot that history consists of a flux in which mythological patterns repeat themselves. Yeats believes that the individual imagination must incarnate those patterns, whereas Pound, like Pater, strives for a receptive sensitivity which allows the universal order to articulate itself. Yeats questions whether this is possible, whether an order will imply itself. "Can impressions that are in part visual, in part metrical, be related like the notes of a symphony; has the author been carried beyond reason by a theoretical conception?"[116] Pound himself was conscious of the problem; he lamented, "I cannot make it cohere," but he remained committed to the extraordinary risk of that enterprise.

Many modern poets hold in common with Pound the ideal of a realist poetics. Working not from a European but from an aggressively American tradition, William Carlos Williams wants a poetry in which there are "no ideas but in things." Building a poetics upon the work of Pound and Williams, the objectivist poets—Zukofsky, Olson—seek to rid the poem of the lyrical interference of the ego, to make man an object among other objects, to make the poem itself an object of reality. Their enterprise involves similar risks and problems to those of Pound. The very reconstitution of meaning the poem invites involves bringing back as a rationalizing principle the ego the poet demands he "wash out." In *Conceptions of Reality in Modern American Poetry*, L. S. Dembo wonders whether radically objectivist theories of perception do not in fact come full circle to a kind of subjectivism, whether "external reality requiring a special mode of perception becomes, in part, internal reality sustained by a particular sensibility."[117] This paradox, he argues, characterizes the objectivist poetics of modern writers. It is a paradox rooted in a reaction to Romanticism which first takes form in Victorian poetry. To escape the limitation of the individual ego, Victorian poets and critics urged scrupulous attention to objects as they really are. But the attempt to compose a poetry of objects often implied, paradoxically, the constituting mind while depriving the poet of the resources the agentive imagination provided.

Jonathan Culler has argued that literary history should be a history of semiological systems, of signification.[118] He offers as an example of such a history the distrust of allegory in Romantic poetry and the return to it in Baudelaire and Flaubert. Culler argues that one can see in Romantic poetry and critical theory, specifically in Coleridge's preference for symbol over allegory, a desire for objects to have immanent meanings. The Romantics use the imagination to protect that signifying relationship. The testimony "I saw" guarantees the immanent meaning of the world I behold. Yet the dependence of the signifying relationship upon the imagination makes it vulnerable as well. The Victorians and the Modernists wished to avoid the vulnerability the individual imagination seemed to impose while they still desired assurance of a symbolic universe in which objects have inherent meanings. The desire to reconstitute an apparent and necessary order in the world of things motivates much poetic theory from that of Ruskin and Arnold to that of Eliot and Pound. Yet the poetry suggest how fragile and difficult an enterprise such a poetics involved. The desire to avoid "arbitrary subjective processes" paradoxically leads to the surrender of certain kinds of control over meaning. The attempt "to see the object as in itself it really is," to follow "objective lines of relation in nature herself," to let the facts "generalize themselves" creates a poetry of ambiguity and indeterminacy precariously poised between objective and subjective organizations of reality. The desire for a poetry of images without interpreting discourse that Hallam articulates and that many Victorian and modern poets share results, paradoxically, in a loss of the objective stability it strives to sustain.

In the last chapter, I suggested that the New Criticism's use of the term "persona" gave critical expression to the contradictions implicit within the form of the dramatic monologue as that form is developed by Modernist poets. In its emphasis on tension and ambiguity, the New Criticism has found a similar way to accommodate the conflicts between subjective and objective organizations of reality that the poetry seeks to sustain. Like the term "persona," the terms "tension," "paradox," and "ambiguity" can be used to control and rationalize various contradictions within post-Romantic poetics. In fact, the New Criticism's conception of the poem as an object which itself generates poetic emotion resembles the way in which Modernist poetics defines the image. And like the poetry, the criticism that stresses the object as an emotional sign independent of interpretive discourse must allow ambiguity as an end in itself.

4

Myth, History, and the Structure of the Long Poem

In *The Spirit of the Age,* John Stuart Mill asserts that the dominant characteristic of his time is a habit of historical comparison.

> The "spirit of the age" is in some measure a novel expression. I do not believe that it is to be met with in any work exceeding fifty years in antiquity. The idea of comparing one's own age with former ages, or with our notion of those which are yet to come, had occurred to philosophers; but it never before was itself the dominant idea of any age.[1]

Many historians have agreed with Mill's judgment. Historicism—the belief that only through an understanding of historical process can man find an explanation of human experience—has so dominated intellectual discourse of the nineteenth and twentieth centuries that it has seemed not one idea among many but the condition of all thought.[2] A philosophical idea of such centrality naturally has a profound impact on literary form.

Much Victorian and Modernist poetry seeks to discover in history a teleology that gives value and direction to past and present. Tennyson, Arnold, Browning, Yeats, Pound, Eliot all strive to apprehend a pattern in history that composes not only a subject but a formal principle for their poetry.[3] The movement of history provides the ultimate objectifying structure through which the poet can transcend the limitations of a merely personal vision, yet the stuff of history—facts, documents, personalities, situations—often seems to reveal only a contextual relativism that denies any teleological pattern. Victorian and

Modernist poetry accordingly often shows conflict between a historical relativism according to which truth depends upon historical perspective and a cosmic point of view toward history which assigns ultimate meaning to historical events.[4] Their work thus displays a contradiction in their attitude toward historical fact similar to the contradiction which I have argued characterizes their use of both personae and objects. On the one hand, they imply that events and values only take meaning from a particular context. On the other hand, they seek in some way to establish an absolute basis of historical valuation, whether it be a positivist science of history, a mythological structure, or even both. This tension in the historical vision of many Victorian and modern poets has had important consequences for the form of their poetry. Victorian and modern poems seek frequently to establish a historical context which they then absorb into some ahistorical structure. In works as different as *The Ring and the Book*, *In Memoriam*, *The Cantos*, and *The Waste Land*, a contextual relativism conflicts with an absolute order independent of the perceived. The fragmentation of narrative form supplies the gap which allows historicism and ahistoricism contradictorily to occupy the same poetic space.

Matthew Arnold's poetry and prose supply important evidence of the tensions that characterize Victorian attitudes toward history. Of all the Victorian poets, Arnold speaks most eloquently of the pain of modernity.[5] The pain arises from a vision of historical process which determines the possibilities of action, of belief, even of feeling, and which, in Arnold's early work, men are powerless to affect. Like many Victorian thinkers, Arnold locates the present between historical eras, "one dead, the other powerless to be born."[6] Modern man's location at a point of historical decline allows him none of the old forms of belief which Arnold feels inspire action and feeling. Yet man, in Arnold's poetry, cannot hasten the new age which will supply new forms of belief because historical process operates independently of individual will. The man sensitive to his historical predicament is therefore condemned to a life of futility whose only palliative is resignation.

Early poems like "Stanzas from the Grande Chartreuse" and "In Memory of the Author of Obermann" express Arnold's sense of helpless entrapment at the wrong historical moment. In the later poem, "Obermann Once More," the character of Obermann articulates Arnold's own early historical determinism. Man needs joy, Obermann asserts, but his historical location keeps him from feeling it.

> ' "Ah, not the emotion of that past,
> Its common hope, were vain!
> Some new such hope must dawn at last,
> Or man must toss in pain.
>
> ' "But now the old is out of date,
> The new is not yet born,
> And who can be *alone* elate,
> While the world lies forlorn?"
>
> 'Then to the wilderness I fled,
> There among Alpine snows
> And pastoral huts I hid my head,
> And sought and found repose.
>
> 'It was not yet the appointed hour.
> Sad, patient, and resigned,
> I watched the crocus fade and flower,
> I felt the sun and wind.
>
> 'The day I lived in was not mine,
> Man gets no second day.
> In dreams I saw the future shine—
> But ah! I could not stay!'

By the time that he composed "Obermann Once More," Arnold had come to reject for his own part the fatalism Obermann voices. After the account of his historical situation I have just quoted, Obermann declares that the appointed hour has at last arrived in Arnold's time and urges Arnold to help bring its hope to others. The poem thus reflects a far greater optimism about the possibilities that man's historical situation offered than Arnold's earlier poetry. Despite the greater optimism of the later poem, however, it presents an equally deterministic vision of man's historical predicament. The older Arnold is fortunate to live at the moment of the new dawn. He can help spread its light, but he could not have brought it about. Its appointed hour had come. The poem offers no consolation to those souls like Obermann or the young Arnold who inhabit moments of historical decline; it offers only a greater optimism about man's postion in the historical cycle. Arnold's poetry sustains a vision throughout of a historicism that determines possibilities of action and feeling.

His prose offers a more complex series of attitudes toward historicism. On the one hand, it reiterates that same sense of the modern, of the power that history holds over action and feeling which I have described in his poetry. On the other hand, it repeatedly appeals to permanent human emotions which exist independently of time and history. The Preface to the 1853 edition of his poems expresses both of these attitudes. The essay depends upon a distinction between the ways in which modern and ancient times foster great literature. Because the modern age lacks moral grandeur and spiritual health, modern civilization does not supply those great actions which so powerfully and delightfully impress the human soul. The heroic temper of ancient times supplied such actions and thus made possible a great literature. Arnold's characterization of modern and ancient literature thus implies a belief that historical process determines the nature of a given literature. But his distinction between modern and ancient also depends upon an idea of great action which exists independently of time. In asking himself what actions are the most excellent, he replies: "Those, certainly, which most powerfully appeal to the great primary human affections: to those elementary feelings which subsist permanently in the race, and which are independent of time. These feelings are permanent and the same; that which interests them is permanent and the same also."[7] Arnold's prescription for poetry—that the poet choose to represent such excellent actions—appears to be an anachronism in the light of his own belief in the determining power of history. His poetics displays a contradiction between historical and ahistorical assumptions. Only the appropriate historical climate fosters the qualities of mind, character, and feeling which produce great literature. Yet the poet inhabiting an unpropitious time must imitate those very actions which his own age cannot foster.

The poems that critics most frequently associate with the principles of the 1853 Preface are "Sohrab and Rustum," "Balder Dead," and *Merope*. Each of these poems takes as its subject restoring a broken generational continuity. In "Sohrab and Rustum" Sohrab attempts to prove his worth to his father, Rustum, who does not even know he exists, by meeting him in combat. In "Balder Dead" Hermod tries to restore Odin's son Balder, the sun god, to life by showing that all things mourn his death. In *Merope* Aepytus returns to regain his rightful position by killing the uncle who had murdered his father, married his mother, and usurped his throne. In each of these poems, the action that Arnold chooses to imitate thus reflects the poetic principle according to which the poem is composed—gaining worth through restoring a broken connection with the past. In "Sohrab and Rustum" and in "Balder Dead," the attempt to restore succession fails. Sohrab is killed by the father he sets out to meet, and Rustum only realizes the identity of his son as Sohrab lies dying. In "Balder Dead" Lok in the shape of the hag Thok refuses to mourn Balder's death. Hel will not release Balder, and the light and joy he brings are lost to the gods. Despite the attempt to reinstate lost values that inspires their composition, both poems thus center upon actions that show the impossibility of restoring a broken succession. In "Sohrab and Rustum" the father kills the son who presents himself on the same terms as a rival. In "Balder Dead" the entire creation will not mourn the dead and restore it to life; one dark and anarchic element rejoices in its passing. The poems in this way show the necessary defeat of the ideal which had inspired them. Although the Preface speaks of the necessity of imitating classical models, even Arnold's poems written in accordance with his classical principles bespeak his surer insight that a connection once broken cannot be restored. His classical poems undermine the poetic principles their composition supposedly illustrates by showing the determining power of historical separation.

Merope is an exception to this pattern. Aepytus does kill his uncle and regain his father's throne. But Clough said perhaps the kindest thing that could be said of *Merope* when he wrote, "I cannot say that I received much natural pleasure from it when I read it."[8] Arnold's own comments on the poem suggest that he undertook it not, as the 1853 Preface declared, to appeal to the great primary human affections, but to avoid certain painful emotions. In a letter to his sister discussing the reception of the poem, he writes: "People do not understand what a temptation there is, if you cannot bear anything not *very good,* to transfer your operations to a region where form is everything. Perfection of a certain kind may there be attained, or at least approached, without knocking yourself to pieces."[9] To a friend Arnold writes of *Merope:* "I am anxious to explain to you that you are not the least bound to like her, as she is calculated rather to inaugurate my Professorship with dignity than to move deeply the present race of *humans.*"[10] The only poem in which Arnold successfully inscribes his classicism was an academic exercise which evades his deepest feelings about history.

Arnold's decision to turn from poetry to criticism acknowledges what his poetry reflects—the futility of the classicism of the 1853 Preface. His poetry throughout confirms a sense that the break with the past is irreparable, that the creative power has lost its life-giving connection with its heroic roots. But in his criticism he finds a way of accommodating his conviction of the determining power of history with his desire for ahistorical touchstones of value that can subsist permanently in the critical consciousness. When he first begins his critical task of disseminating the ideas that will make a great literature once again possible, he mediates uneasily between definitions of the truth which emphasize its objectivity and those which emphasize its relativity. We can see the conflict in this passage from "The Function of Criticism at the Present Time."

> It is the business of the critical power, as I said in the words already quoted, "in all branches of knowledge, theology, philosophy, history, art, science, to see the object as in itself it really is." Thus it tends, at last, to make an intellectual situation of which the creative power can profitably avail itself. It tends to establish an order of ideas, if not absolutely true, yet true by comparison with that which it displaces; to make the best ideas prevail.[11]

The best ideas are those which "see the object as in itself it really is," but they are not "absolutely true, yet true by comparison." As the essay progresses, Arnold becomes more emphatic about criticism's detachment from the world of practice, and the definition of criticism becomes less dependent upon its historical location. Later in the essay Arnold tells us that criticism's best spiritual work is to lead man toward perfection "by making his mind dwell upon what is excellent in itself, and the absolute beauty and fitness of things."[12] But despite his attempt to separate criticism from the world of practice and associate it with unchanging excellence, Arnold keeps returning to the world of history to stress the importance of the function of criticism at and for the present time. Arnold wishes both to escape and to seize his historical moment. His ambivalence toward history creates tension between the definitions of criticism that the essay offers.

In the idea of culture that he develops in *Culture and Anarchy,* Arnold achieves a more comfortable accommodation between historical and ahistorical constructs of cultural value since culture is both a historical process and an ahistorical absolute.[13] He sustains this contradiction by nominalizing the progressives which define culture's activity. "Not a having and a resting, but a growing and a becoming, is the character of perfection as culture conceives it."[14] By reifying culture's dynamic activity, Arnold can maintain its historical location while he can manipulate it as a fixed entity which provides a stable location of human value.

Arnold's final major essay on poetics, "The Study of Poetry," gives up the attempt to mediate between historical and absolute estimates of literary value. Although Arnold feels that we may be misled by our study of the context of a writer's achievement to make a historical estimate of his value, he insists that we must not fall prey to this temptation but make instead the real estimate, "the only true one." In making a real estimate of a poet, we will determine "if he is a real classic, if his work belongs to the class of the very best (for this is the true and right meaning of the word *classic, classical*)."[15] We will be aided in our judgment by touchstones, lines of poetry which reveal their value independently of the context either of the poem in which they appear or of the age in which they were written.

The touchstones that Arnold discovers in "The Study of Poetry" enable him to escape the consciousness of the determining power of history he found so burdensome, and it is interesting how closely they approach Pater's aesthetic appreciations of the intense moments art offers, as T. S. Eliot realized.[16] But Arnold's notion of culture is finally more significant because it sustains the conflicting pressures upon him. His poetry failed to find a way to accommodate those pressures, but his criticism, much as he dreamed, fostered ideas which enabled modern poets to succeed where Arnold failed. Eliot, Pound, and Yeats each use touchstones from the past to construct a culture that is at once a historical process and an ahistorical pattern. Arnold's poetry offered little that the Modernists could use, but his criticism, as we shall see, strikingly anticipates many of the ideological strategies through which they could write poems, in Pound's words, "including history."[17]

Unlike Arnold, Browning did discover ways of making his poetry sustain at once a historical relativism and a knowledge of truth free of the biases of historical perspective. His ability to sustain such a contradiction depends in part upon his use of historical fact as the raw material for his poetry. He values fact for a number of interesting and complex reasons. Although he locates essential reality in the way man thinks and feels, the existential psychology of being, the poet can only begin to approach that psychology through the facts which evidence it. Browning values the old yellow book from which he composes *The Ring and the Book* because it preserves

> pure crude fact
> Secreted from man's life when hearts beat hard,
> And brains, high-blooded, ticked two centuries since.
>
> (I,35–37)

Some fifty lines later Browning repeats the words I have just quoted. "The thing's restorative," he exclaims (I,89). The facts, the documents, enable the poet to resuscitate the human life that time extinguishes. Browning would like to believe that the facts can speak for themselves, declare their own value. He boasts that the yellow book contains "absolutely truth, / Fanciless fact, the documents indeed . . . real summed-up circumstance" (I,143–44, 146). Browning finds to his distress that documents contain the maze of lies, the conceit of truth that human speech is heir to. The documents thus pose the problem Browning's historical poetry must solve: how to resuscitate the past so that the facts do indeed declare their own meaning, how to enable truth "to take its own part as truth should, / Sufficient, self-sustaining" (I,373–74).

Browning discovers that to make truth take its own part he must add "something of mine" (I,462). In the controlling metaphor of *The Ring and the Book,* that something of mine is the alloy which enables the pure gold of fact to "bear hammer and be firm to file" (I,463). Once the ring is complete, however, a spurt of acid removes the alloy, and the gold, now crafted into a ring, regains its original purity. There has been a great deal of critical debate about the meaning of the metaphor.[18] Critics' inability to agree on what Browning meant suggests an incoherence in the metaphor itself. The metaphor at one and the same time admits and denies the shaping power of the poet. It at first makes the truth dependent upon the poet's informing power. Slivers of pure gold are "mere oozings from the mire," unable to sustain shape (I,11). They need the alloy which the poet's imagination supplies in order to be crafted into a ring. Yet once the ring is made, Browning attempts to detach the imagination from the final product. The completed ring contains no trace of the alloy: "Oh, there's repristination!" (I,23). Although Browning gives the imagination a central formative role, he detaches it at the end to stress both the objective nature of the truth with which the poet deals and of the artifice which he constructs. He even tries to give the imagination itself objective status: "Fancy with fact is just one fact the more" (I,464). Later he asks, "Is fiction which makes the fact alive, fact too?" (I,706). The metaphor seems unclear because it sustains a contradiction: the poet forms materials which bear no trace of his forming.

Browning contains this contradiction in his definition of the poet's activity as resuscitation. The poet, by an act of identification, of empathetic understanding, brings the dead to life. Describing his recreation of the story of *The Ring and the Book,* Browning writes:

> The life in me abolished the death of things,
> Deep calling unto deep: as then and there
> Acted itself over again once more
> The tragic piece.
>
> (I,520–23)

Browning's verbs here suggest the paradox he wishes to enforce. Although the life in him abolishes the death of things, the piece then "acted itself." Once galvanized into life, it possesses its original power of self-determination. Later in the first book, Browning describes the creative process as bringing corpses to life. Browning quotes an imaginary mage, although he describes the magician as "stopping midway short of truth, / And resting on a lie" (I,743–44). The mage first asserts "man makes not man." He continues:

"Yet by a special gift, an art of arts,
More insight and more outsight and much more
Will to use both of these than boast my mates,
I can detach from me, commission forth
Half of my soul; which in its pilgrimage
O'er old unwandered waste ways of the world,
May chance upon some fragment of a whole,
Rag of flesh, scrap of bone in dim disuse,
Smoking flax that fed fire once: prompt therein
I enter, spark-like, put old powers to play,
Push lines out to the limit, lead forth last
(By a moonrise through a ruin of a crypt)
What shall be mistily seen, murmuringly heard,
Mistakenly felt: then write my name with Faust's!"

(I,746–59)

By writing his name with Faust's, Browning makes his resuscitation of corpses an act of black magic, an inappropriate usurpation of the divine privilege of creating life. But Browning then dismisses the Faustian analogy to choose that of Elisha and thus sanctify the act of "mimic creation."

Oh Faust, why Faust? Was not Elisha once?—
Who bade them lay his staff on a corpse-face.
There was no voice, no hearing: he went in
Therefore, and shut the door upon them twain,
And prayed unto the Lord: and he went up
And lay upon the corpse, dead on the couch,
And put his mouth upon its mouth, his eyes
Upon its eyes, his hands upon its hands,
And stretched him on the flesh; the flesh waxed warm:
And he returned, walked to and fro the house,
And went up, stretched him on the flesh again,
And the eyes opened. 'Tis a credible feat
With the right man and way.

(I,760–72)

Like Elisha, the poet brings historical figures back to life by bestowing his life and breath upon them. By choosing Elisha as his model and not Faust, the poet makes himself an instrument of divine power, not a usurper of divine privilege. In his resuscitation, he does not make a ghost from historical debris but restores the dead to life.

Browning's conception of history as the reenactment of past experience resembles that of a number of nineteenth- and twentieth-century philosophers of history. A strong current in nineteenth-century English and German historiography emphasizes comprehension of the past through existential recreation of individual personalities typical of the developing human consciousness. In his essay on Boswell's *Life of Johnson,* Carlyle writes:

> The thing I want to see is not Redbook Lists, and Court Calendars, and Parliamentary Registers, but the LIFE OF MAN in England: what men did, thought, suffered, enjoyed; the form, especially the spirit, of their terrestrial existence, its outward environment, its inward principle; *how* and *what* it was; whence it proceeded, whither it was tending.[19]

Morse Peckham and Roger Sharrock both argue the similarity of Browning's conception of history to that of a number of nineteenth- and twentieth-century historiographers, particularly Leopold von Ranke, who urged a similar existential understanding of past experience.[20] The culmination of this movement in nineteenth-century historiography occurs in the work of Dilthey, Croce, and Collingwood, all of whom share the assumption that the historian attains knowledge of the past by empathetically rethinking in his own consciousness those mind products he confronts as the remnants of the past. Collingwood quotes Croce approvingly: "Do you wish to understand the true history of a neolithic Ligurian or Sicilian? Try, if you can, to become a neolithic Ligurian or Sicilian in your mind.'"[21]

The historians I have just mentioned all show themselves aware of the limitations the historian's own consciousness may impose upon his reenactment of the past. Ranke is aware of the distortion his own personal bias imposes on his evaluations. Collingwood writes that "the historian himself, together with the here-and-now which forms the total body of evidence available to him, is a part of the process he is studying, has his own place in that process, and can see it only from the point of view which at this present moment he occupies within it."[22] Browning differs from this historiographical tradition in seeking to avoid the problem his own point of view might impose upon his materials.[23] Nonetheless, he repeatedly shows an uneasy awareness of the potential problem. In one of the most striking images from *The Ring and the Book*, the pope recalls the trial of the dead Pope Formosus by his successor Pope Stephen VII. Stephen exhumes the body of the dead pope, sets it upon the papal throne clothed in its vestures and subjects it to trial and condemnation. The image offers a grotesque parody of Browning's images in the first book in which the poet brings the dead to life. The poet may not bring the dead back like Elisha but set up a corpse on a throne for private and mistaken reasons. And he may never know his error. The pope who succeeds Stephen reverses Stephen's judgment; the next pope reaffirms Stephen's right; the last pronouncement of the church declares Formosus to be a holy man. The pope dismisses the story with a shudder of humility and horror. One senses that Browning would like to do the same despite the uneasy consciousness the image reflects that the alloy may be all in all, that there is no repristination. The image of the ring allows him to deny the possibility of the poet's bias. The renovating wash of water removes any personal adulteration: "I disappeared; the book grew all in all" (I,687).

The form that Browning uses to effect the disappearance of the poet from his book is the dramatic monologue. The dramatic monologue contains the contradiction Browning wishes to sustain. It enables him to breathe his life into historical figures while it maintains the illusion of his detachment from his materials. The past, inspired by his breath, seems to declare its own meaning without his interference. The form is valuable not only for the voice that it gives the past but for the silence that it gives the poet. In the beginning of *Sordello*, Browning expresses his desire for the form most of his subsequent poetry was to take. He asserts that the ideal way to present his materials would be a story bodied forth:

> By making speak, myself kept out of view,
> The very man as he was wont to do,
> And leaving you to say the rest for him. . . .
> I should delight in watching first to last
> His progress as you watch it, not a whit
> More in the secret than yourselves who sit
> Fresh-chapleted to listen.
>
> (I,15–17, 22–25)

Sordello is an important precedent for Browning's subsequent poetic achievement in using an enormous amount of historical documentation to provide objective validation for the subjective biography of which the poem consists, but it does not realize the desire for the author's invisibility that Browning here expresses. Browning speaks a great deal in *Sordello,* sustaining an explicit parallel, unusual in his work, between Sordello's poetic enterprise and his own. But this parallel gives the figure of the poet at once too much prominence and too little privilege. It subjects Browning to the historical limitations which situate and determine Sordello's career. As the lines I have just quoted attest, Browning wished his own poetry to be free from the historical limitation of his own manipulations. The dramatic monologue allows him to recreate the historical personality who engages him while it seems to secure his own freedom from historical bias.

Despite his desire to free himself from the limitations of historical bias, Browning was very much preoccupied with the ways in which the historical period in which one lives conditions perception. Like many of his contemporaries, he wanted to define the feeling of particular historical moments—the coming of the Renaissance as in "Fra Lippo Lippi," or the coming of Christianity as in "Cleon" or "The Epistle from Karshish." As Robert Langbaum has argued, many of Browning's dramatic monologues seek to project a historical point of view according to which moral judgments are absorbed into historical characterization.[24] We are less interested, for example, in the moral evil of the duke of "My Last Duchess" or of the bishop at St. Praxed's Church than we are in the way in which that evil characterizes the preoccupations of their age.

Like Arnold, Browning feels that historical periods manifest a zeitgeist, revealed in art, religion, life-style. The zeitgeist seems to have a natural life-span; it is born, it decays, and dies, to be replaced by the germ of a new culture. As Arnold does, Browning conceives of the movement of history as an evolutionary process with a logic independent of the human actors who manifest it. Unlike Arnold, however, Browning tends not to give his characters historical self-consciousness (with the great exception of the pope in *The Ring and the Book*). Like Cleon or Karshish, they inhabit moments which they do not understand. Their historical location imposes a blindness upon them which keeps them from understanding the movement of history. Browning's structuring of the poem, however, implies the very understanding his characters lack. He often locates poems at moments of historical transition where a new culture offers possibilities of a richer life the old culture denies. History at one and the same time imposes a blindness but brings the light. Characters are historically deluded, but history is always offering enlarged possibilities of vision.

Browning's historical poems thus embody a contradiction. He at once represents man's consciousness as determined by history and implies a point outside of history from which that consciousness can be judged and the structure of history comprehended. Once again, it is the dramatic monologue that allows Browning to contain the contradiction, for the form can at once display the historical conditions of the speaker's understanding and maintain the fiction that the poet does not suffer similar limitation. The poem—or the whole body of poems—can thus imply a structure of historical progression operating independently of the poet.

The Ring and the Book is Browning's most significant experiment in implying such a total structure through the very historical relativism that seems to preclude it. In the poem he sets nine partial views limited by history and by character in a frame which implies the possibility of a holistic view absorbing each particular angle. In lines that allude to Shelley, Browning imagines the red, green, and blue whirling into white (I,1362–64). Somewhere exists a vantage where contradictions are resolved and the total scheme revealed. But that vantage may not exist within the ken of any human observer. *The Ring and the Book* is extraordinary in the skeptical possibilities of knowledge the poem entertains within the holistic structure it envisions. The pope voices the most extreme vision of any character in Browning of the blindness that history, character, and language impose. He contemplates with horror the possibility that history may not be progressive; he recalls the spectacle of subjecting a corpse to a personal judgment which is then proclaimed as holy writ. He sees language as man's curse, the inevitable lie. He finally rejects the most skeptical possibilities he entertains. Man can and must judge, trusting that the spark from the divine which he has been given enables him to weigh the seed of an act. Nonetheless, the pope's speculations about the limitations that

history, personality, and language impose upon judgment cannot be so easily dismissed. In the pope's monologue, Browning
introduces possibilities of judging the poem's own meaning
which implicate the poet himself, questioning his ability to
achieve the neutrality and truth to which he aspires.

In order to delimit the skeptical possibilities that the pope suggests, Browning develops a concept of art in Books I and XII not
subject to the conditions of human speech. Through the image
of the ring, Browning maintains that the poet can subtract himself and his impurities from the finished book. In the conclusion
to Book XII, Browning claims that art can penetrate where
human speech cannot: "it is the glory and good of Art, / That
Art remains the one way possible / Of speaking truth"
(XII,838–40). Art can thus achieve that vantage point which implies the perfect round, the one truth.

> But Art,—wherein man nowise speaks to men,
> Only to mankind,—Art may tell a truth
> Obliquely, do the thing shall breed the thought,
> Nor wrong the thought, missing the mediate word.
>
> (XII,854–57)

As Browning here asserts, art can tell the truth through obliquity. The great discovery of *The Ring and the Book,* the characteristic of the poem that makes it so important a precedent for
Modernist poetry, consists in the obliquity whereby the poet implies a structure rationalizing and containing the particular fragments the poem presents. Through the pluralism of its form,
the poem reconciles its historical relativism with its dream of
supplying a vision of the whole. The poem supplies a historical
context for each of the particular angles of vision that it presents, while it implies that the whole work of art gives us the total
vision which we would like to achieve. The discontinuity of
form, the absence of the poet as a continuous, historically situ-
ated narrator makes such an achievement possible. By omitting
yet implying an encompassing vision, the poem can at once contain historical and ahistorical constructions of reality.

With Browning and Arnold, Tennyson feels a conflict between a fidelity to a historicism that recognizes the way in which
the context of any individual action determines standards for its
judgment and a desire to reveal the providential design which

determines the meaning of each individual action in accordance with a divine purpose.[25] This conflict finds very different expression in the forms of Tennyson's two major long poems, *In Memoriam* and *Idylls of the King.* Each individual section of *In Memoriam* represents a separate response to Hallam's death in Tennyson's psychological history. Tennyson claims for them the justification and authenticity of particular experience while he disclaims a larger synthetic purpose. Sorrow dare not trust "a larger lay," "But rather loosens from the lip / Short swallow-flights of song, that dip / Their wings in tears, and skim away" (XLVIII). The fragmentary nature of *In Memoriam* seems to reflect a fidelity to the diverse individual forms of sorrow that Tennyson describes, and indeed it does. But as in *The Ring and the Book,* the discontinuity of the poem, its division into sections which each offers only a single angle of vision, creates spaces in which another kind of construction can take place. Despite the despair of its early sections, the poem ultimately arrives at a faith in the providential design of history. All is "toil cooperant to an end" (CXXVIII). There is "one far-off divine event, / To which the whole creation moves" (Epilogue). The poet, located in history as he is, cannot articulate that end or that event.

> Our little systems have their day;
>> They have their day and cease to be:
>> They are but broken lights of thee,
> And Thou, O Lord, art more than they.
>
> (Prologue)

Man's limitations keep him from seeing the perfect whole, but the fragmentary nature of the poem allows Tennyson to imply the structure that he cannot articulate. Some structure does contain and rationalize the particular moments of vision that the individual sections describe. As in *The Ring and the Book,* the discontinuity of the poem's form allows Tennyson at one and the same time to emphasize the integrity of the particular historical experience and to imply a containing whole independent of the direction of the poet.[26]

Maud uses the fragmentation of narrative form in a similar way. Each of the lyrics articulates a phase of the protagonist's experience. In the spaces between the lyrics, Tennyson merely implies the narrative design which connects and contains the particular moments that the poem depicts. T. S. Eliot realized the potential richness of Tennyson's experiments with form in *Maud* and *In Memoriam*. After describing Tennyson's difficulty with narrative, Eliot writes:

> But in *Maud* and in *In Memoriam*, Tennyson is doing what every conscious artist does, turning his limitations to good purpose. *Maud* consists of a few very beautiful lyrics . . . around which the semblance of a dramatic situation has been constructed with the greatest metrical virtuosity.[27]

Eliot finds the form of *In Memoriam* an even finer accomplishment. *In Memoriam* "is unique: it is a long poem made by putting together lyrics."[28] Eliot's praise singles out the characteristic of the poem that anticipates Modernist poetry. Like Browning in *The Ring and the Book*, Tennyson realized that by effacing the continuous narrative structure of the long poem, he could maintain a fidelity to particular angles of vision while he could imply a single design beyond the vantage point of even the poet.

In the *Idylls of the King*, Tennyson evolves a different way of reconciling individual historical experience with the providential design of history. *In Memoriam* succeeds by what it does not say. The one being who has moved in both temporal and eternal worlds, Hallam, cannot speak: he is the absent center around which the poem moves. While his absence motivates the poem's despair, only his absence can provoke the dream of history's significance. In *Idylls of the King*, Tennyson creates a character in King Arthur who provides what is in *In Memoriam* the unspoken intersection of the temporal and the eternal. Arthur is both a character in the human drama of the *Idylls* and the spiritual authority who reveals the divine model for human action in history. The two roles fit together least comfortably in the portrayal of Arthur's relationship to Guinevere. In the scene at Almesbury in "Guinevere" in which Arthur passes judgment upon her, the ideological authority with which Arthur invests himself gives him a petulance that hardly accords with the dignity and force that the poem claims for his character. Arthur promises Guinevere that he will send men to guard her.

Fear not: thou shalt be guarded till my death.
Howbeit I know, if ancient prophecies
Have erred not, that I march to meet my doom.
Thou hast not made my life so sweet to me,
That I the King should greatly care to live;
For thou hast spoilt the purpose of my life.
Bear with me for the last time while I show,
Even for thy sake, the sin which thou hast sinned.

(445–52)

Arthur then proceeds to explain the design he tried to realize
and the way in which Guinevere has ruined it. It is easy to dis-
miss the passage as an instance of Tennyson's obtrusive moralizing, but the problem that the passage reflects is in fact more
significant. The difficulties that the poem has with the character
of Arthur result from Tennyson's choice to articulate a connection between human psychology and historical design that much
of his other work leaves implicit.

Much as Tennyson uses the figure of Arthur to give a more
fixed relationship to psychology and spiritual authority than exists in other of his poems, so he uses the Arthurian legends to
project a far more fixed sense of historical design. The poem
continually plays off against each other a character's present experience and the end we know will come. The last lines of "Lancelot and Elaine" read:

So groaned Sir Lancelot in remorseful pain,
Not knowing he should die a holy man.

(1417–18)

The poem introduces Modred with notice of his end.

But Modred laid his ear beside the doors,
And there half-heard; the same that afterward
Struck for the throne, and striking found his doom.

("The Coming of Arthur," 322–25)

The first idyll is full of implications and statements of the end of
the order that has only just begun. As Arthur takes Excalibur,
Merlin says, " 'Take thou and strike! the time to cast away / Is yet
far-off' " (306–7). Although Tennyson does not say what will
happen after Arthur's death and although he is careful not to

attach his authority to any of the poem's magical tokens, he nonetheless frequently uses his narrative authority to state the end to which a character will come. In much of his other poetry, as we have seen, Tennyson quite deliberately surrenders this authority, preferring to imply a structure that no individual can articulate. *In Memoriam* and *Maud,* much like *The Ring and the Book,* disavow certain kinds of poetic authority to authorize an objective structure beyond the poet's control. In the *Idylls of the King,* Tennyson seeks a principle of authority more similar to the one that Arnold seeks in his classical poems. The shape of a legend gives a shape to history whose design the poet can project.

As in Arnold's classical poems, the shape that Tennyson projects is of decline, of a broken contract with the past. A. Dwight Culler has argued that the poem's concern with decline expresses Tennyson's own anxiety about his belatedness as a poet, that Arthur's failure is his failure, that the poem even in articulating the Arthurian ideal as something already lost at its beginning dramatizes poetry's and Tennyson's inability to recreate the city built to music.[29] Culler's reading of the poem suggests an important connection between Tennyson's use of Arthurian legend and Arnold's classicism. In the very use of past legendary materials to give stability and authority to the patterns they describe, both poets inscribe the necessary break with the past. Like Arnold's classical poems, the *Idylls of the King* was not useful for the Modernists, despite its accomplishment. The explicitness that Tennyson gives to its principle of order and authority makes the *Idylls* at once more vulnerable and more finished than the poems the Modernists found more useful models. Nonetheless, the *Idylls,* like Arnold's poetry, give poignant expression to a predicament that the Modernists shared—how the poet can use knowledge of a culture which reveals both his own belatedness and his inevitably broken connection with the past.

In a review of *Quia Pauper Amavi,* T. S. Eliot defines the "sustained purpose" which motivates Pound's work as "historical method." He goes on to explain of what that method consists:

> The historical method is, of course, the one which suits Mr. Pound's temperament; it is also a conscious and consistent application of a procedure suggested by Browning, which Mr. Pound applies more consciously and consistently than

Browning did. Most poets grasp their own time, the life of
the world as it stirs before their eyes, at one convulsion or
not at all. But they have no method for closing in upon it.
Mr. Pound's method is indirect and one extremely difficult
to pursue. As the present is no more than the present existence, the present significance, of the entire past, Mr.
Pound proceeds by acquiring the entire past; and when the
entire past is acquired, the constituents fall into place and
the present is revealed. Such a method involves immense
capacities of learning and of dominating one's learning,
and the peculiarity of expressing oneself through historical
masks.[30]

Although Eliot here is describing Pound's early poetry, his description indicates the direction of Pound's subsequent development, for it is the enterprise not only of *Quia Pauper Amavi* but of
The Cantos (of which the first version of the first three had already been published) to reveal the present by reconstituting the
entire past in the most ambitious and extensive juxtaposition of
historical masks that poetry had contained.

Eliot here gives credit to Browning as the poet whose works
suggested the possibility of the method. As we have seen, Pound
generously credits Browning's influence upon him. He calls *The
Ring and the Book* "serious experimentation,"[31] but the poem of
Browning's which seems to have been most important to Pound
in the genesis of *The Cantos* is *Sordello*. He begins the first Ur-
Canto with irritation that *Sordello* had preempted an exciting poetic possibility: "Hang it all, there can be but the one 'Sordello.'"

Sordello was important to Pound for a number of reasons. In
Gaudier-Brzeska, Pound calls *Sordello* "one of the finest *masks* ever
presented."[32] Much of the appeal of the poem to Pound must
have lain in the way in which Browning's conception of Sordello
involved many of Pound's own preoccupations as a poet. Dedi-
cated to a mystic conception of sexuality, trying at once to re-
form literary language and effect a political revolution, Sordello
involves himself in many of the same ideals as the young Pound.
The poem records two crises in poetic election: Sordello's and
Browning's. Sordello, alive at the wrong historical moment to
realize his ideals and with a more grandiose conception of himself than circumstances seem to confirm, fails at the mission he
attempts. The poem suggests by its ironic references to Browning's own poetic vocation and its realization in the poem *Sordello*

that Browning may be likewise misplaced. Pound's similar situation at the crisis of poetic election that beginning *The Cantos* must have posed would make *Sordello* appear one of the finest masks ever created.

There were formal reasons for the poem's appeal as well. First, its difficulty was attractive to Pound. Although Pound praised it in the *ABC of Reading* for "limpidity of narration and lucidity of sound," he elsewhere calls it "unreadable."[33] Even more important than its difficulty is its use of a dense texture of historical detail to materialize, locate, and validate a spiritual condition. But the poem most strikingly anticipates Pound's technique when it manipulates a parallel between past and present in a historical overlayering unique in Victorian poetry.[34] When Pound refers to *Sordello* in *The Cantos,* he refers to the moments of historical overlayering in the poem. These moments occur when Browning relates his own doubts about poetic vocation to Sordello's story. Canto III, for example, "I sat upon the Dogana's steps," begins with a reference to lines from *Sordello* which record such a crisis. Browning breaks off Sordello's story at a point where he meditates upon the disproportion of life and work, the very partial evidence Sordello's poems give of his intense spiritual life. He then turns aside from his sotry to question the adequacy of his own muse—a peasant girl who comes to image the entire world of poetic subjects:

> I muse this on a ruined palace-step
> At Venice: why should I break off, nor sit
> Longer upon my step, exhaust the fit
> England gave birth to! Who's adorable
> Enough reclaim a—no Sordello's Will
> Alack!—be queen to me? That Bassanese
> Busied among her smoking fruit-boats?
>
> (III,676–82)

In a resolution typical of his poetry, Browning's decision to accept a world in its partial good reveals its divine grace, and he resolves to continue the poem.

Pound's crisis takes a somewhat different form. He wonders not whether the world offers adequate inspiration for poetry but whether there remains enough space for his literary enterprise. He resolves this crisis of poetic election as he does whenever such crises arise in *The Cantos* by reference to the continual magical reincarnation of the pagan gods. I will quote the passage from the Ur-Cantos from which Canto III derives because it makes clearer the association between ideas.

> Your palace step?
> My stone seat was the Dogana's vulgarest curb,
> And there were not "those girls," there was one flare,
> One face, 'twas all I ever saw, but it was real . . .
> And I can no more say what shape it was . . .
> But she was young, too young.
> True, it was Venice.
> And at Florian's under the North arcade
> I have seen other faces, and had my rolls for breakfast,
> Drifted at night and seen the lit, gilt cross-beams
> Glare from the Morosini.
> And for what its worth
> I have my background; and you had your background,
> Watched "the soul," Sordello's soul, flare up
> And lap up life, and leap "to th'Empyrean";
> Worked out the form, meditative, semi-dramatic,
> Semi-epic story; and what's left?
> Pre-Daun-Chauder? Pre-Boccacio? Not Arnaut,
> Not Uc St Circ.
>
> Gods float in the azure air,
> Bright gods and Tuscan, back before dew was shed;
> Is it a world like Puvis'?
> Never so pale, my friend,
> 'Tis the first-light—not half-light—Panisks
> And oak-girls and the Maelids have all the wood;
> Our olive Sirmio
> Lies in its burnished mirror, and the Mounts Balde and Riva
> Are alive with song, and all the leaves are full of voices.
> *"Non e fuggi."*
> "It is not gone." Metastasio
> Is right, we have that world about us.[35]

Here Browning serves Pound much as Sordello serves Browning—as an image of poetic aspiration, as one who wants to cast his vision in a new form but can only see the exhausted poetic possibilities of the past. Pound overcomes his anxiety about "what's left" by assuring himself that "Gods float in the azure air," that "we have that world about us." In the reworking of this passage in Canto III, Pound follows it with a declaration of his participation in the poetic tradition: "My Cid rode up to Burgos," although with few resources, exiled from his home.

In the Ur-Cantos, the crisis of poetic election continues in a way that recalls the crisis in Browning's own work. After a much more expansive section recalling the gods and men's songs to them, Pound writes:

> What have I of this life?
>   Or even of Guido?
> A pleasant lie that I knew *Or San Michaele,*
> Believe the tomb he leapt was Julia Laeta's,
> Do not even know which sword he'd with him in the street-
>   charge.
> I have but smelt this life, a whiff of it,
> The box of scented wood
> Recalls cathedrals.   Shall I claim;
> Confuse my own phantastikon
> Or say the filmy shell that circumscribes me
> Contains the actual sun;
>   confuse the thing I see
> With actual gods behind me?[36]

Pound's words here recall Browning's fear of the distorting film his own subjectivity imposes. Earlier Pound criticizes Browning for the historical distortion *Sordello* contains.

> Ghosts move about me patched with histories.
> You had your business: to set out so much thought,
> So much emotion, and call the lot "Sordello."
> Worth the evasion, the setting figures up
> And breathing life upon them.[37]

Both of these passages suggest that one of Pound's major fears as he began *The Cantos* was that historical masks may be only a displacement of his own subjectivity. The image that first occurs in the Ur-Cantos, that first appears in *The Cantos* proper in Canto III, to recur several times, which embodies this fear of Pound's, is the story of Pedro and Ignez da Castro.[38] Pedro sets up the corpse of his murdered queen on the throne and compels the very courtiers who had murdered her to do her homage. The image recalls Browning's image in the pope's monologue in *The Ring and the Book* of the dead Pope Formosus disinterred, robed, and brought to judgment, and the images suggest similar anxieties. Is the construction of historical masks a deluded displacement of the poet's own phantastikon with no relation to the realities of historical judgment?

Like Browning, Pound seeks to resolve this problem by minimizing his presence within the poetic discourse he creates. One of the striking differences between the Ur-Cantos and *The Cantos* is the reduction of the poet's role as presenter of his materials. Like Browning, Pound wishes to create the illusion of an unmediated presence of history. The poem "Near Perigord," published in *Lustra* in 1915, both recalls Browning's imagination of historical reality and anticipates the method of *The Cantos*. In the poem, Pound tries to discover some key that will enable him to interpret the troubadour Bertrans's utterances in a way that will reveal the spirit that informed them. In the first section of the poem, Pound tries to sift through the historical facts contained in the little evidence that survives. Encountering only frustration, he next tries to recreate the past through fiction. In the final section of the poem, Pound realizes his quest much as Browning gains access to history in *The Ring and the Book;* he recreates the subjective sense of the historical moment by imagining Bertrans's soliloquizing. It is true that the final words of the poem, "a broken bundle of mirrors," qualify the success of the entire effort. Much as Bertrans cannot know Maent, we cannot know Bertrans. But we come closest to him in the moment of existential empathy when the poet seems to disappear from the poem. Like Browning, Pound thus uses the dramatic monologue to achieve the illusion of history's unmediated presence. "By making speak, myself kept out of view, / The very man as he was wont to do," Pound can detach himself from the problems of historical and personal bias that his own voice implies. The same desire that leads Pound to speak in Bertrans's voice leads him as well to minimize his narrative presence in *The Cantos*.

Together with the minimization of his own role as narrator, Pound develops a positivist theory of history whereby significant facts are sufficient carriers of their own meaning. Pound explains this theory in "I Gather the Limbs of Osiris." He calls it "the method of Luminous Detail." Certain facts "give one a sudden insight into circumjacent conditions, into their causes, their effects, into sequence, and law." He continues:

In the history of the development of civilization or of literature, we come upon such interpreting detail. A few dozen

facts of this nature give us intelligence of a period—a kind
of intelligence not to be gathered from a great array of
facts of the other sort. These facts are hard to find. They
are swift and easy of transmission. They govern knowledge
as the switchboard governs an electric circuit.

These facts carry their own significance. The poet, like the scientist, does not need to interpret. He needs only to discover the facts and present them.

The artist seeks out the luminous detail and presents it. He
does not comment. His work remains the permanent basis
of psychology and metaphysics. Each historian will 'have
ideas'—presumably different from other historians—imperfect inductions, varying as the fashions, but the luminous details remain unaltered.[39]

In the method of luminous detail, Pound outlines a positivist
theory of history to which he holds throughout his poetic career.
The writing of history consists of two things: ascertaining facts
and framing laws. The facts are immediately ascertained by sensory perception. The laws are framed by generalizing from
these facts by induction. Each fact can be ascertained by a separate act of cognition; thus the total field of the knowable can be
cut up into an infinity of separate facts. Furthermore, facts are
independent of the knower. Thus the historian need fear no
distortion his subjectivity might inflict; he only gives the facts
without comment.

The inadequacies of this method as a theory of history are as
obvious as its advantages to Pound as a poetics. It enables him to
do what Browning desired: make the facts speak for themselves.
He can extend the ideal of the self-sufficient image that had
motivated his early poetry into the world of history and provide
nothing less than an objectively based theory of civilization and
culture in a poetry that is decisively modern. A collage of appropriately selected images will carry their own significance, imply
general laws. Furthermore, the method of luminous detail frees
the poet from the burden of self-presentation and the distortions
of vision it implies. The method assures that the poet presents not
his own *phantastikon* but the actual sun. Just as Browning resolved the crisis in poetic identity that *Sordello* represents by absenting himself from the poem, so Pound resolves the crisis that

the Ur-Cantos reflect by minimizing his own role as poetic narrator, presenting luminous details without judgment or comment.

Much as Browning does not value "pure crude fact" for itself but for the residue it preserves of spirit "secreted from man's life when hearts beat hard," so Pound values luminous details for the evidence they supply of a man's spiritual condition and consequently that of the culture he shares. Personal and artistic styles provide an index to the health of a surrounding society. Thus Pound can use a letter from Jefferson asking for a gardener who can play the French horn (Canto XXI) as a sign of both Jefferson's moral quality and the moral quality of the nation he leads.

Pound of course does not locate a poem within a single consciousness but cuts from consciousness to consciousness, from historical narration to fragments of quotations from literary and philosophical works to images, often of nature or of gods in nature. Through this historical collage, Pound constitutes a universal cultural memory which knows itself by its differences from the very elements which compose it. Pound's constitution of this consciousness contains within it a contradiction, however, similar to the contradiction which characterizes Browning's poetic enterprise. *The Cantos* contain two contradictory modes of historiography which attempt at one and the same time to compose historical location and to free man from it.[40] Pound attempts a feat which should be impossible: to write a poem composed of history and of individual consciousness. As Browning does, he accomplishes this extraordinary contradiction by placing an existential historicism within a positivist framework. He allows the two to coexist by the method of fragmentation and juxtaposition he evolves. By virtue of its gaps and absences, his poem contains contradictory ideologies within the same poetic space.

One of these ideologies is a historicism, similar to Browning's and to the modern historicist tradition, whereby historical data give man the occasion for reliving in his own mind the spiritual activity which originally produced them. We know different ages and individuals by entering imaginatively into their points of view. We understand this spiritual activity most profoundly when we understand the historical conditions which surround it. By recreating the material conditions of Sigismundo's existence, for example, we can reconstruct his point of view. Our own spiritual life makes it possible for us to reconstruct the past in this way. We infuse our life into dead materials. These materials in turn enlarge our own consciousness. In constituting the past, we compose ourselves. We thus come to know both our own significance and the present significance of the entire past. By eliminating a controlling voice, Pound can compose this general cultural consciousness. *The Cantos* efface individual subjectivity to reconstitute a universal historical subjectivity.

In conflict with this existential historicism, however, is a positivist morphology of history which undertakes to induce historical laws by the collection of appropriate specimens. The success of the Monte dei Paschi, the failure of the Medici Bank are the samples on which the indictment of usury is based in Canto 45. Pound often juxtaposes such historical laws with self-sufficient natural signatures in order to suggest the kinship of the two. In Canto 51, for example, Pound juxtaposes a recapitulation of the usury canto with instructions for creating a particular fisherman's fly:

Usury is against Nature's increase.
Whores for Eleusis;
Under usury no stone is cut smooth
Peasant has no gain from his sheep herd
      Blue dun; number 2 in most rivers
for dark days, when it is cold
A starling's wing will give you the colour
or duck widgeon, if you take feather from under the wing
Let the body be of blue fox fur, or a water rat's
or grey squirrel's. Take this with a portion of mohair
and a cock's hackle for legs.
12th of March to 2nd of April
Hen pheasant's feather does for a fly,
green tail, the wings flat on the body
Dark fur from a hare's ear for a body
a green shaded partridge feather
      grizzled yellow cock's hackle
green wax; harl from a peacock's tail
bright lower body; about the size of pin
the head should be. can be fished from seven a.m.
till eleven; at which time the brown marsh fly comes on.
As long as the brown continues, no fish will take Granham.

The fly here represents a principle of production learned from nature, based on exact observation, whereas usury is an artificial increase not based upon labor. Underlying the contrast between usury and the fly, however, is a similarity in the mode of signature which nature and history leave. Careful observation of specimens enables one to frame the laws that will alike classify fish, flies, and cultures, nature, human artifacts, and historical events. The canto shows the same assimilation of culture to nature as Fenollosa's "Essay on the Chinese Written Character." The Chinese history cantos, which follow directly on the canto I have just quoted, offer an exemplum of a society based on nature's signatures. The emphasis Pound places on Chinese characters and the positivist science of history he attempts to embody in *The Cantos* reflect a similar desire to see culture as a set of natural signs implying their own laws, a morphology of history.

Of course, such a construction is ahistorical. It implies a point outside of history from which laws and patterns can be seen, a laboratory where history exists spread out in a timeless space which is the artifact of the poem. This ahistorical conception of culture can coexist with the historicism I have previously described by virtue of the gaps which are the determining characteristic of the poem's form. The pieces are there, without a controlling narrator, as a mode both of historical experience and of scientific induction. Pound develops a potential that is present in Browning of using discontinuities in poetic form to permit simultaneous historical and ahistorical interpretation of the same poetic events. The Pisan Cantos are the one section of the poem that escapes the contradiction I have been describing, because in them Pound presents himself as a historically based consciousness composing history and vision. They succeed far better as history and as poetry, as a result escaping the dogmatism and chaos that characterize Pound's poetic enterprise at its worst because they portray the force of desire which makes the poem's contradictions cohere.

The discontinuities in *The Cantos* allow many contradictions to exist beyond the one I have described. There is a tension in the poem between what Hugh Kenner calls metamorphosis and slither.[41] The universe at one and the same time operates according to a principle of magical transformation which manifests the divine bounty of creation and a principle of slippage, dissolution of everything to mud. There is furthermore a tension between atomism, in which everything is particular, a law unto itself, existing once and once only, and connection, in

which things comprise an eternal order perpetually reincarnat-
ing itself. The poem thus moves in the rhythm of history in
which everything dies and the rhythm of myth in which everything is always regenerated. In all of these tensions, Pound uses
the indeterminacy of the poem's form to imply at once a modern
sense of disorder and an overarching single order. In one of the
great paradoxes of the development of modern literature,
Pound introduces the most radical possibilities of form, allowing
a greater indeterminacy of meaning than poetry had yet contained, in order to incorporate possibilities of order the very
structure of his poetry seems to preclude.

Although Eliot and Pound evolve similar techniques of both
structure and fragmentation for the long poem, they have very
different views of historical possibility. Pound dreams of a uto-
pian ideal accessible to a culture which maintains the clarity and
economy of nature's signs in its operations. For Pound, human
beings can act effectively in history; Eliot despairs of the possibility of their doing so. Although Eliot believes that the course
of history is determined, that "what might have been and what
has been / Point to one end, which is always present," man cannot control results by willed action. Gerontion articulates the
sense of futility which characterizes Eliot's vision of historical
possibility in his early poetry.

>   Think now
> History has many cunning passages, contrived corridors
> And issues, deceives with whispering ambitions,
> Guides us by vanities. Think now
> She gives when our attention is distracted
> And what she gives, gives with such supple confusions
> That the giving famishes the craving. Gives too late
> What's not believed in, or if still believed,
> In memory only, reconsidered passion. Gives too soon
> Into weak hands, what's thought can be dispensed with
> Till the refusal propagates a fear. Think
> Neither fear nor courage saves us. Unnatural vices
> Are fathered by our heroism. Virtues
> Are forced upon us by our impudent crimes.

That Gerontion uses this vision of history to rationalize his own
refusal of "closer contact" only confirms the vision of history he
articulates. Even the disillusioned contemplation of historical

futility deceives with a cunning passage which justifies Gerontion's refusal to act.

Throughout his career, Eliot sought ways of transcending this
vision of history, of redeeming time. The first method he pur-
sued he calls "the mythical method." In a review of Joyce's *Ulysses,* he writes:

> In using the myth, in manipulating a continuous parallel
> between contemporaneity and antiquity, Mr. Joyce is pur-
> suing a method which others must pursue after him. They
> will not be imitators, any more than the scientist who uses
> the discoveries of an Einstein in pursuing his own, inde-
> pendent, further investigations. It is simply a way of con-
> trolling, of ordering, of giving a shape and a significance to
> the immense panorama of futility and anarchy which is
> contemporary history. . . . Instead of narrative method, we
> may now use the mythical method.[42]

Although Eliot does not mention his own poetry in the review,
his description of "the mythical method" has obvious relevance
to *The Waste Land,* published the year before. Indeed, Eliot's description applies far more accurately to *The Waste Land* than it
does to *Ulysses.* Joyce's work contains a narrative that is coherent
without reference to the episodic structure of the *Odyssey,* whereas *The Waste Land* depends upon the structure of myth to supply
the place of narrative connection.

Eliot's essay on *In Memoriam,* written in 1936, thirteen years
after the review of *Ulysses,* shows Eliot's continuing concern with
ways of structuring a long poem that provide an alternative to
"narrative method." Eliot's sensitivity to Tennyson's experiments with form stems from a similar difficulty with narrative.
Just as he observes of Tennyson, Eliot himself had little gift for
narrative, probably because of a similar discomfort with agency
and will. Few of Eliot's characters act; they refuse the opportunity to act like Prufrock, Gerontion, and the speaker of "Portrait of a Lady," or they observe and suffer like Tiresias. Eliot's
sense of the futility of historical action is only one manifestation
of a discomfort with all categories of agency which shows itself in
both his poetry and his criticism, as I have argued. Eliot's difficulty with action does not pose formal problems in his shorter
poems, for in them, like Tennyson, he can use lyric and image to
sustain a mood for an appropriate length of time. But the struc-

ture of the long poem, as the essay on Tennyson and Eliot's own difficulties with the draft of *The Waste Land* reflect, poses far greater problems.

Precisely in the matter of the structure of the long poem, Eliot could use Tennyson's discoveries. The essay on *In Memoriam* has been related to the composition of *The Four Quartets*.[43] Indeed, Eliot was working on the *Quartets* at the time of the composition of the essay, and the two poems have much in common. But *In Memoriam* has much in common with *The Waste Land* as well.[44] Both are elegies for a dead friend which confess a psychological disintegration mirrored in apocalyptic visions of God's failure to redeem time by revelation. Like Tennyson, Eliot discovers that he can construct a long poem "by putting together lyrics," one might even say "around which the semblance of a dramatic situation has been constructed with the greatest metrical virtuosity."[45] In both poems, the speaker seeks to surrender his will, while the poet insinuates a redeeming providential shape to time.

Tennyson uses evolutionary philosophy to imply such a shape; Eliot uses what he calls the mythical method. Myth allows Eliot a rigorous condensation while it absolves him of the narrative task which the long poem has traditionally undertaken. Such a discovery has philosophical as well as technical implications. It allows Eliot to sustain the sense of the futility of historical action while it offers a redeeming rhythm which manifests itself in history but operates independently of the will of any historical actor.[46] The mythical method allows Eliot not only a technical solution to the problem of sustaining order in a long imagistic poem without a continuous narrative, but also a philosophical resolution that at once sustains and transcends his feeling of the futility of action. The characters of *The Waste Land*— Mme. Sosostris, the woman whose portrait opens "A Game of Chess," Lil, Mr. Eugenides, the typist and the clerk, Elizabeth and Leicester, La Pia, Phlebus the Phoenician, the Fisher King— all manifest the mythical rhythm that controls the poem despite the ignorance, the vanities, of their individual desires and their inability to act effectively.

Eliot thus sustains a contradiction in *The Waste Land* in many ways similar to the contradiction that Pound sustains in *The Cantos*. On the one hand, the poem presents an immense panorama of individual historical acts, isolated from each other, of indeterminate end, yet pushing toward chaos and disintegration. On the other hand, the poem implies a redeeming rhythm that works through them bringing hope of regeneration. Both divine and natural, the rhythm possesses the inevitability and universality of not one creed but the entire body of myth. As in *The Cantos*, it is the omission of explanatory and connecting matter, the gaps in the poem's form, that allow this contradiction to exist. The gaps at once reinforce the poem's atomism, the sense it communicates of the chaos and anarchy of contemporary history, while they supply the space in which a mythical structure, implied in the poem's characters and events, can be erected. The very fact that the myth is not stated by the poet but implied by structure, by titles, and verified by scholarly apparatus gives it an inevitable universality the poet's voice could not achieve.

In contrast to Pound in *The Cantos*, Eliot asserts that *The Waste Land* has a central consciousness in the figure of Tiresias. But Tiresias merely contains without resolving the contradictions I have noted. He at once participates in the individual acts which compose history while he insinuates some universal structure which contains them without differentiating them. Because Tiresias has "forsuffered all," he provides a center for the poem without defining the force of desire that would make its contradictions cohere. Like Pound, Eliot seeks to submerge the shape of that individual desire.[47] Tiresias functions much like the mythical method itself: he contains contradictions without either making them cohere in a specific way or resolving them.

Eliot thus uses the mythical method to insinuate an ahistorical mythical rhythm within the events of history. Like Pound, he uses quotations from literature to sustain both a historicist and an ahistoricist vision. Cultural artifacts evidence the consciousness of past and present. The allusion to Spenser in "The Fire Sermon," for example, "Sweet Thames, run softly while I end my song," suggests at once a cultural and poetic integration in the Renaissance and our modern distance from that harmony. At the same time that the quotations and allusions in *The Waste Land* construct the present through its consciousness of the past, they constitute an ideal order in which all literature composes a timeless unity.

In its use of the past to compose the present, *The Waste Land*, like *The Cantos*, displays a radical solution to modern literature's ambivalence toward its own belatedness. Nietzsche describes the

Modernist's position most eloquently. Modern man needs rescue from the disease of history because of his consciousness that he must live in a historical or twilit atmosphere, because of the fear that he can retain none of his youthful hopes and powers. One solution to the problem that Nietzsche describes is to wipe out history, to forget everything in order to do something.[48] Another solution is the one that Arnold's career reflects—the abandonment of poetry in recognition that we live in a critical, not a creative, age. But Pound and Eliot suggest yet a third solution—that a new art can result precisely from an extreme self-consciousness of cultural history.[49] In this way they create a poetry that enacts Arnold's definition of culture. The continual exercise of the critical intelligence, composing one's historical moment by accumulating the best that has been known and thought, does not merely construct a medium which makes poetry possible; it composes that poetry.

Much like Arnold's definition of culture, Eliot's and Pound's use of tradition to claim a new place in the history of literature accommodates a tension between historical and ahistorical understandings of art. "Tradition and the Individual Talent" displays this tension:

> what happens when a new work of art is created is something that happens simultaneously to all the works of art which preceded it. The existing monuments form an ideal order among themselves, which is modified by the introduction of the new (the really new) work of art among them. The existing order is complete before the new work arrives; for order to persist after the supervention of novelty, the *whole* existing order must be, if ever so slightly, altered; and so the relations, proportions, values of each work of art toward the whole are readjusted; and this is conformity between the old and the new.[50]

The passage I have quoted shows a tension between an ahistoricist and a historicist construction of literary history. On the one hand, the present gives the past meaning in reconstructing its order so that our understanding of literary history is always a historical consciousness centered in our understanding of the present generation. On the other hand, works of art at any moment form a timeless ideal order independent of any perceiving agent. The verbs of the passage suggest Eliot's attempt to maintain a historical order independent of historical agency. Much like his description of the creative process from the same essay, his definition of the way in which tradition is established avoids agency. Eliot uses the passive voice and verbs like "happens," "forms" to suggest a process operating independently of individual determination. Much like Arnold's definition of culture, Eliot's definition of tradition at once proposes itself as a historical process and a timeless absolute, a set of accumulating touchstones by which we can orient ourselves. Furthermore, it fulfills much the same ideological function as Arnold's definition of culture. It contains within itself both the historicism fundamental to the modern understanding of society and an ahistoricism that resists the pressure of history.

It was Eliot's and Pound's genius to devise a poetic technique that could simultaneously incorporate this historicism and ahistoricism. In the fragmented cultural collage structured by implied mythical rhythms which they both in different ways evolved, they found a way of constituting a historical understanding of the present and escaping it in a timeless spatial mythical order. They at once stand within history and imply a point outside of history from which its order can be perceived. By effacing a controlling author, by fragmenting materials, they allow the two visions to coexist within the same literary work.

Eliot's conversion to Christianity brought changes in his attitude toward history that made the form of his later poetry different from that of his early work. Whereas Pound remains committed to his historical method to the end of his career, making even more extreme demands of it as *The Cantos* progress through *Rock Drill* and *Thrones*, Eliot finds a theological center for the point outside of history which gives history meaning. Although the *Four Quartets* repeats the five-part structure of *The Waste Land* and depends on the insinuation of a divine connecting force to structure its lyrical units, it is far more explicit than Eliot's early poetry in articulating the philosophical principles upon which its vision of time and history rests.

Despite the striking shift that his conversion to Christianity seems to reflect and the changes in his poetry which it brought, Eliot's ideal of Christian culture repeats the formulations of much of his early work. His pattern reverses Arnold's, a fact which may explain his hostility to Arnold's ideals. Whereas Arnold, as Eliot lamented, tried to make poetry occupy the place of

religion,[51] Eliot used formulations similar to his early definitions
of poetic experience to describe Christian culture. In an authen-
tically Christian culture, the activities of different members of
society compose a harmony at once profound and unconscious.
But in a society experiencing the disintegration of culture, "religious thought and practice, philosophy and art, all tend to become isolated areas cultivated by groups in no communication
with each other."[52] Eliot's definition of culture echoes his earlier
concern with the dissociation of sensibility and its effect on poetry. Likewise Eliot's concern with the unconsciousness of culture
recalls his attempt to imply a unifying structure in his early poetry that cannot be willed or articulated. In *Notes toward the Definition of Culture,* he writes:

> Culture is the one thing that we cannot deliberately aim at.
> It is the product of a variety of more or less harmonious
> activities, each pursued for its own sake: the artist must
> concentrate upon his canvas, the poet upon his typewriter,
> the civil servant upon the just settlement of particular
> problems as they present themselves upon his desk, each
> according to the situation in which he finds himself.[53]

The way in which culture emerges as "the unconscious background of all our planning"[54] that reveals the order we enact
but cannot will suggests the way in which myth operates in his
early poetry. Eliot's concern with Christian culture only seems to
represent a radical break with his early symbolist experimentation; both in fact reflect a desire for a unifying structure to reveal itself independently of the will of any single participant.
This desire results paradoxically in both the most radical experiments in discontinuity of poetic form and a conservative social
orthodoxy. It is true that *The Waste Land* and *The Cantos* are very
different poems from *In Memorian* and *The Ring and the Book.*
Nonetheless, they share with them the desire to imply a historical structure which seems to exist independently of the control
of the poet. As traditional as the Victorian poems are in relationship to the modern ones, they begin to use discontinuity in a
similar way to maintain a fidelity to the particular historical moment beyond which no man can see and to imply the total structure within which he moves.

"The Packet for Ezra Pound" that Yeats places at the beginning of *A Vision* suggests a consciousness on Yeats's part that he

was posing a theory of history that in some way countered and paralleled the system implied in *The Cantos.* Yeats shares Eliot's and Pound's attempt to combine a historicist understanding of man's implication within history with a point beyond history from which history can be ordered. The determinism of the philosophy of history that he presents in *A Vision,* its domination by mythical metaphors, the use of art as an escape from history all have similarities to Eliot's and Pound's historical enterprise. But Yeats's way of poeticizing his concern with history differs from that of Eliot and Pound. He does not try to efface the poet's agency within history but centers his poetry on the poet, alternately enacting and contemplating the history which possesses him and which he possesses.

Like Eliot and Pound, Yeats seeks a point outside of history from which he can understand the process that is history. *A Vision* supplies that point from which the structure of history reveals itself and enables him "to hold in a single thought reality and justice."[55] Although Yeats claims the authority of the spirits for his vision, he remarks twice in "The Packet for Ezra Pound" on the remarkable coincidence between his views of history and Spengler's, thus offering validation from another source for his dates and metaphors. The coincidence illustrates the strange partnership between scientific positivism and mythological systems of history. Both alike seek to establish an objectively based morphology of history which can identify the life cycles of cultures and thus predict the future. This coincidence in fundamental aim explains why Yeats (and Pound) can claim with little sense of contradiction both positivist and theological support for the same propositions.

The determinism of Yeats's theory of history, however, exists in tension with a commitment to the freedom of the individual. Thomas Whitaker's book *Swan and Shadow: Yeats's Dialogue with History* concerns itself with this tension. Whitaker quotes a 1930 diary entry in which Yeats articulates the poles of the tension. "History seems to me a human drama, keeping the classical unities by a clear division of its epochs, turning one way or the other because this man hates or that man loves. . . . Yet the drama has its plot, and this plot ordained character and passions and exists for their sake."[56] Another passage from the 1930 diary suggests the relationship between *A Vision* and the individual poems: "History is necessity until it takes fire in some one's head and becomes freedom or virtue."[57] *A Vision* instructs the reader in the idea of historical necessity with which Yeats was inspired; the poems dramatize the fire that history takes in someone's head to become freedom or virtue.

The stress that Yeats places upon human agency indicates an important difference between the poetry he writes concerning history and the poetry of Eliot and Pound. Eliot and Pound, as we have seen, strive in different ways to efface the poet's agency in composing history. But Yeats triumphantly proclaims his role in summoning the historical and mythological figures from which he constructs the past that he inhabits. "The Tower," for example, repeatedly stresses the poet's role in making the history that he passes on.

> I pace upon the battlements and stare
> On the foundations of a house, or where
> Tree, like a sooty finger, starts from the earth;
> And send imagination forth
> Under the day's declining beam, and call
> Images and memories
> From ruin or from ancient trees,
> For I would ask a question of them all.

Even poems in which the speaker is a more passive recipient of a vision of historical reality strive not to establish the objective validity of the vision but to dramatize the speaker's attempt to ask a question of what he sees. After the initial image of the swan above Leda, "Leda and the Swan" proceeds through a series of questions, each more consequential and unanswerable than the last.

> How can those terrified vague fingers push
> The feathered glory from her loosening thighs?
> And how can body, laid in that white rush,
> But feel the strange heart beating where it lies?
>
> . . . .
>
>   Being so caught up,
> So mastered by the brute blood of the air,
> Did she put on his knowledge with his power
> Before the indifferent beak could let her drop?

"The Second Coming" likewise ends with a question.

> And what rough beast, its hour come round at last,
> Slouches towards Bethlehem to be born?

One could gloss both of these poems from *A Vision,* and many scholars have, but such a gloss might well miss the point. The speaker does not assert as a matter of historical science the moment of the end and beginning of a cycle but asks as a horrified question whether the moment of historical crisis he inhabits could portend an apocalypse whose ultimate meaning he cannot predict. Yeats stresses the knowledge his location in history withholds as well as gives; he does not know what rough beast slouches toward Bethlehem. The surety that the poem offers is not an objective validation of historical cycles but the speaker's desire for some apocalyptic revelation, however horrible, to order the chaos he inhabits.

> Surely some revelation is at hand;
> Surely the Second Coming is at hand.

The repetition of *surely* stresses not historical reality but the speaker's desire that some end might be.

In addition to emphasizing the agency of both poet and speaker, Yeats emphasizes the particular historical location of his poems. He presents his meditations upon history from a specific point of view within history—September 1913, Easter 1916, 1919. The specific location of his poems stresses the historical relativity of the state of mind they dramatize. Yeats does not choose to write a long poem which represents his idea of history. In light of the detail and complexity of the historical schematization he evolves in *A Vision,* his commitment to the lyric is particularly significant because it reflects the value he places upon man's subjective power to give the moment in which he lives imaginative form. Eliot and Pound each seek release from the waste of history by implying a redeeming mythological rhythm beyond the control of the poet's agency, and they each evolve a form of the long poem to incarnate that rhythm. Yeats, on the other hand, finds redemption from the waste of history in the poet's power to image even the destruction he sees. Much as Eliot's and Pound's evolution of the form of the long poem reflects their attempt to efface the poet's personality within a more objective matrix, so Yeats's commitment to the lyric implies his attempt to emphasize the personality even when confronted by the power of history.

The personality in Yeats nonetheless operates within an objective matrix supplied by myth and history. The image which horrifies the speaker of "The Second Coming" arises from *Spiritus Mundi*. Yeats felt that his use of the facts of Irish history gave his poetry an objectivity that Blake's, for example, lacked.[58] Yet the objective matrix takes form from the fire of the individual imagination. The second section of "Nineteen Hundred and Nineteen" shows the way in which the imagination dominates even visions of history's destruction.

> When Loie Fuller's Chinese dancers enwound
> A shining web, a floating ribbon of cloth,
> It seemed that a dragon of air
> Had fallen among dancers, had whirled them round
> Or hurried them off on its furious path;
> So the Platonic Year
> Whirls out new right and wrong,
> Whirls in the old instead;
> All men are dancers and their tread
> Goes to the barbarous clangour of a gong.

The dragon in the first section of the poem has been an image of the brutality and terror of contemporary history. The conception of the Platonic Year gives that brutality and terror the inevitable authority of historical cycle. But the idea of the Platonic Year depends upon the image of Loie Fuller's Chinese dancers. The image not only gives a beauty and grace to the dragon but controls the image by artifice created by a powerful imagination much as the poem itself controls the destruction and brutality of the history it confronts. The control is not an easy one; the poem takes its tension and its greatness from the dialectical relationship among its images. But it continually stresses the genesis of those images in men's conceptions of their predicament.

The stress the poem places upon human constructions of reality encourages the reader to create a different kind of relationship between the sections of the poem than I think either Eliot or Pound encourages in their poetry. Like many of Yeats's major lyrics, "Nineteen Hundred and Nineteen" consists of a number of sections which are not obviously continuous with one another as either narrative or argument. Yeats thus uses gaps between disconnected lyrical units much as Pound and Eliot do. But each of the sections of "Nineteen Hundred and Nineteen" except the last represents very explicitly the imagination's response to man's historical predicament. Section one concerns the relationship between what we once thought and what we now see. Section two presents the image I have just quoted of Loie Fuller's Chinese dancers. In section three the speaker contemplates some poet's comparison of the soul to a swan and tries to possess that image as his own. Section four compares our talk of seven years ago with today's images. Section five invites our mockery of the great, the wise, the good, and the mockers. Only section six, the poem's last section, presents an image not mediated or generated by human agency. The poem's stress on human supposition, construction, and imagining encourages us to make psychological, not mythological, connections between its sections. Of course, one can make psychological connections between the sections of *The Waste Land* or *The Cantos,* but those are not the ideal links the poems seek to imply. Yeats stresses psychological connections so that the image which ends the poem seems to incarnate myth within the individual historical imagination rather than claim for it an impersonal reality which subsumes the individual and history. For all the similarities between Yeats's idea of history and the ideas of Pound and Eliot, his poetry presents a very different way of knowing history than his prose. As in his development of mask and symbol, in his representation of history Yeats seeks to sustain the centrality of the individual imagination.

Although Yeats shares the historicist interest of much Victorian and modern poetry, he remains true to a Romantic heritage. The radical Modernist techniques which Eliot and Pound evolve in order to write a long poem containing history paradoxically place them in a closer relationship to the Victorian poetic enterprise. They evolve poetic techniques that sustain the contradictions in Victorian attempts to find a poetry in history. The poetry indeed is radically different from Victorian poetry. But its most extreme differences—the fragmentation, the effacement of a controlling consciousness—are motivated in large part by an effort to sustain the very contradictions in historical vision which characterize the Victorian poetic enterprise. "The mythical method," "the method of luminous detail" fulfill the dream Browning had of writing a poem about history which transcends the biases of historical consciousness, of presenting the real without the interfering presence of the poet, of revealing the pattern in history through history. And they accomplished what Arnold prophesied in his prose—the unification of culture as a historical process with culture as an ideal and timeless touchstone of human excellence.

5
Modernism and Anti-Victorianism

In my final chapter I shall discuss a problem which my argument for the continuity of Victorian and Modernist poetics inevitably poses; given the relationships I have described, what explains the sense which Modernist poets and critics share that Modernism represents a sharp break with the Victorian tradition? If Modernist poetry has such strong affinities with that of the Victorians, why do the major Modernist poets repeatedly and emphatically assert that their work makes a radical break with Victorian poetry and poetics? In this chapter I shall pose a number of answers to this question, some of which assess the complex of affinities and disjunctions relating Victorian and modern poetry, others of which define how modern literature characteristically represents its relationship to history. My argument will finally lead me to ask about the value and function of periodization both for the poets I am studying and for ourselves as teachers and scholars of literary history.

I will begin by analyzing exactly what Modernist poets were criticizing in Victorian poetry. Yeats, Pound, and Eliot share a remarkably consistent view of the faults of the Victorians. Their criticisms tend to fall into two categories: they attack what they see as the empty rhetoric of Victorian poetry, and they deplore a habit of moral discursiveness which continually interposes itself between moments of lyric inspiration. In his Introduction to *The Oxford Book of Modern Verse*, Yeats characterizes the revolt against Victorianism by those very charges:

> The revolt against Victorianism meant to the young poet
> a revolt against irrelevant descriptions of nature, the scien-

tific and moral discursiveness of *In Memoriam*—'When he should have been broken-hearted', said Verlaine, 'he had many reminiscences'—the political eloquence of Swinburne, the psychological curiosity of Browning, and the poetical diction of everybody.[1]

In "Modern Poetry" Yeats describes the way in which the impurities of Victorian poetry dissipated the lyric intensity he and his contemporaries sought.

> In the Victorian era the most famous poetry was often a passage in a poem of some length, a poem full of thoughts that might have been expressed in prose. A short lyric seemed an accident, an interruption amid more serious work. Somebody has quoted Browning as saying that he could have written many lyrics had he thought them worth the trouble.[2]

Pound associates Victorianism with "the opalescent word, the rhetorical tradition."[3] He feels that the Victorians lack precision, that they fail at "explicit rendering, be it of external nature, or of emotion." When he calls the nineteenth century "a rather blurry, messy sort of a period, a rather sentimentalistic, mannerish sort of a period," he means that it lacks the precision of the eyewitness's account, that it relies upon clichés of rhetoric and emotion. Furthermore, it had made poetry the vehicle, "the ox-cart and post-chaise for transmitting thoughts poetic or otherwise."[4] In his famous phrase the "dissociation of sensibility," Eliot describes the discursiveness with which Victorian poets reflect upon feeling. Tennyson and Browning lack "direct sensuous apprehension of thought"; "they do not feel their thought as immediately as the odour of a rose." Like all poets after the dissociation set in, "they thought and felt by fits, unbalanced."[5] This dissociation of sensibility makes them dependent upon a rhetoric to represent feeling and thought which distances them from immediate experience. The Victorian poetic tradition can thus logically culminate for Eliot in Swinburne. In the verse of Swinburne, "the object has ceased to exist, because the meaning is merely the hallucination of meaning, because language, uprooted, has adapted itself to an independent life of atmospheric nourishment." Although Eliot grants Swinburne a kind of genius, he announces his preference for the language which is "struggling to digest and express new objects, new groups of objects, new feelings, new aspects."[6]

Admittedly, the rhetoric of modern poetry differs considerably from that of Victorian poetry, and these differences have been frequently analyzed.[7] Although Modernist poets use the rhetorical resources of Victorian poetry far more extensively than they admit,[8] they also evolve different conventions for representing emotion. With their evolution of these conventions, however, comes a denial of the rhetorical nature of their own poetic language. They make their criticisms of Victorian rhetoric in the context of a poetics which claims a transparent representation of thought and feeling. Eliot opposes his criticism of the dissociated sensibility of the nineteenth century to his praise of metaphysical poetry, where there is "direct sensuous apprehension of thought, or a recreation of thought into feeling."[9] Pound contrasts the Victorians with Daniel and Cavalcanti, who achieve the "explicit rendering" which the Victorians lack. "Their testimony is of the eyewitness, their symptoms are first hand."[10] Yeats does not share Eliot's and Pound's emphasis upon poetry's transparent recreation of experience, but he always makes his criticism of the "impurity" of the Victorians in the context of explaining his desire for a pure poetry of lyrical essences. As Yeats admits, opposition to Victorian rhetorical moral fervor becomes opposition to all rhetoric.[11]

The claim that changes in poetic style do away with rhetoric has roots in Romanticism. Moreover, one strain of Victorian poetics, as I have shown in chapter 2, anticipates modern poetry in its stress on the transparent recreation of sense experience. Yet Modernists find models for the freedom from rhetoric and the transparent communication of emotional experience not in the nineteenth-century tradition to which they seem obviously related but in Catullus, the Jacobeans, the troubadours, the Chinese. By locating their models in such distant places, the Modernists are involved, much like the Victorians in their construction of medievalism, in creating a myth of lost origins. They choose periods with congenial stylistic conventions, like the conceit, which they can in some way appropriate, but it is hardly the conventional nature of the poetry that they praise. Rather, they locate in it an essentially Romantic ideal of transparent recreation of sense experience from which poetry has subsequently fallen because of its entrapment in "perdamnable rhetoric."[12] Their own poetry, by doing away with the rhetorical tradition, will reconstitute that lost immediacy and transparency. The rhetoric of the immediate past is so apparent it threatens the modern poet's own enterprise because it exposes the distance between representation and experience. He therefore dismisses it as inauthentic, a departure from that lost presence he recreates. The very commitment that Yeats, Eliot, and Pound each makes to writing a poem of pure reality creates antagonism to the immediate past. The past discloses "impurity," "dissociation," "perdamnable rhetoric." The desire to constitute an unmediated presence which characterizes so much Modernist poetry motivates poets to exaggerate the break with history.

Many other factors motivate that exaggeration as well. One is a change in reading codes. In *Middlemarch,* Dorothea Brooke articulates an assumption that could serve as a paradigm for Victorian attitudes toward reading literature as well as interpreting the world: "The right conclusion is there all the same, though I am unable to see it."[13] Despite the fact that a number of Victorian writers—Browning, Swinburne, Meredith—produce obscure and difficult texts, contemporary criticism of the period assumed not only that literature should provide answers to important problems but that it does. Although Victorian criticism became increasingly tolerant of difficulty in poetry, it never abandoned its confidence that literary texts supply right conclusions about experience. Browning's critical reputation during the Victorian period provides a good index to Victorian attitudes toward the obscurity and interpretability of literary texts. Reviewers criticized not only Browning's early narrative poems but all of his poetry through *Men and Women* for obscurity. The 1855 reviews of *Men and Women,* for example, criticized the volume for extravagant license, madness, mysticism, a lack of artistic conscience in the moral mission of the artist, which was to state solutions of moral problems clearly. Even Swinburne and Ruskin criticized the volume for its obscurity. By 1864, however, when *Dramatis Personae* was published, critical expectations had changed. Browning's style was praised for its complexity, its subtlety, its truth and authenticity.[14] Tennyson's contemporary reputation provides a reverse image of Browning's. In the forties and fifties he was praised for the very universality and clarity of moral statement which, it was felt, Browning lacked. *Maud,* however, published in the same year as *Men and Women,* was

criticized on the same grounds as Browning's volume, one re-
viewer complaining that Tennyson should have omitted either
one vowel or the other from the title. By the 1870s, when
Browning's reputation was at its height, the reaction against
Tennyson had set in. His poetry was criticized for being too simple in conception, artificially limited and refined, unresponsive
to the complexities of human psychology.[15] Despite the increasing tolerance that Victorian criticism showed for difficulty in poetry, however, it did not abandon Dorothea Brooke's faith that
the right conclusion lay there somewhere if only one could see it.
In 1881 the Browning Society was founded not only on the recognition of the difficulty of Browning's poetry but with the confidence that poetry provides right conclusions about experience
if only we can figure them out.

Modernist poets try to create a different set of expectations
about the act of reading. In "The Metaphysical Poets," Eliot
writes:

> Poets in our civilization, as it exists at present, must be *diffi-*
> *cult.* Our civilization comprehends great variety and com-
> plexity, and this variety and complexity, playing upon a
> refined sensibility, must produce various and complex re-
> sults. The poet must become more and more comprehen-
> sive, more allusive, more indirect, in order to force, to
> dislocate if necessary, language into his meaning.[16]

The difficulty that Eliot tells us we must expect does not resolve
itself easily into a single moral attitude. Pound opens Canto 46
with an attack on the reader who expects a "lesson" whereby he
can "get through hell in a hurry."[17] Rather than a lesson, modern poetry offers the reader a strenuous activity of re-combina-
tion, of re-experience, which itself justifies the act of reading. In
the Preface to *Anabasis* that I have already quoted in chapter 3,
Eliot defends Xenophon's omission of "explanatory and connecting matter" in a way that could well describe both his own
poetic method and Pound's method in *The Cantos.* According to
Eliot, this abbreviation lets the sequence of images coalesce into
a single intense impression. In order to experience this impression appropriately, the reader must allow the images "to fall into
his memory successively without questioning the reasonableness
of each at the moment; so that, at the end, a total effect is produced."[18] Eliot here never mentions morality or ultimate con-

clusions; rather, poetry offers a "total effect," a sequence of impressions whose logic the reader can re-experience and thus understand.

The ways in which Eliot, Pound, and Yeats emphasize the complexity and difficulty of poetic texts while they disparage expectations any reader might have for a "lesson" reflect an important change in the codes by which we read. Despite their common delight in the explication of obscurity, *Paideuma* approaches Pound with a very different spirit than the Browning Society brought to Browning. Nonetheless, Modernist criticisms of Victorian didacticism, like their criticisms of Victorian rhetoric, at once articulate a Romantic ideal of the way that poetry presents experience and express fears of its failure. Eliot's definition of the act of reading, whereby the reader allows the images to impress themselves upon him in order to experience the "total effect," has precedents in Victorian poetics and roots in Romanticism.[19] It forms the basis of Hallam's definition of modern poetry, and it resembles Pater's understanding of aesthetic experience. Its source is ultimately the Romantic belief that poetry offers exercise to the entire sensibility, that it brings man to a profound experience of the unity of the affections, a unity threatened by the scientific rationalism of the age. When we find this belief articulated in Wordsworth, in Coleridge, in Shelley, we find poetry associated with the experience of wholeness and other uses of the intelligence—most importantly science—associated with division. But beginning with Keats and extending through Hallam and Pater, the poetry which offers experience to the entire sensibility is opposed to another kind of poetry which interrupts such unified experience to address the reason. Keats and Hallam make Wordsworth the example of such misplaced didacticism; Pater finds an important example of the disruption of the analytic intelligence in Coleridge.[20]

When Eliot, Pound, and Yeats argue that poetry provides a unique experience of the unity of man's faculties, when they decry the disruptions of the analytic intellect, they are thus articulating a Romantic definition of the unique powers of poetry.[21] When they criticize the misplaced didacticism of the Victorians, seeing in it a failure to understand poetry's power to create experience of a unified sensibility, they make an argument similar to the one that we find in Keats, in Hallam, and in Pater.[22] The similarity of nineteenth- and twentieth-century arguments for a poetry of unified sensibility suggests that poets of both centuries experienced similar pressures toward division and responded to them in similar ways. The antididacticism of both centuries expresses at once a nostalgia for a unified sensibility and a defense against the demand for explicit statement of moral values in art. Tennyson's friend, R. W. Trench, told the poet, "Tennyson, we cannot live in Art," and Tennyson wrote "The Palace of Art" in response.[23] The conflict between the principles of Hallam's essay and the moral and social responsibilities for art that the poem proposes reflects a conflict which Tennyson had to resolve between poetry's moral and aesthetic functions. Browning and Arnold also had to confront the pressure toward didacticism central to Victorian poetics. Tennyson, Browning, and Arnold each develops an increasingly didactic stance in the course of his career, while the poets and critics of the aesthetic revolt develop a poetics which again emphasizes poetry's exercise of the entire sensibility.

Modernists criticized the conflicting aesthetic and moral claims under which Victorian poets labored, but their criticism of the conflict does not mean that they did not experience it. Despite their attack on late nineteenth-century aestheticism, Modernist poets continue the revolt against Victorian didacticism that characterizes the poetry and criticism of the end of the century. In this way early Modernism seems less a break with the movement toward art for art's sake than a development of it. Despite their early aestheticism, however, the chief Modernists develop increasingly explicit social programs which they articulate in their poetry as well as in their criticism. Like the Victorians they criticize for misplaced philosophizing, they develop increasingly didactic stances in their poetry. Their development suggests that they experienced an uncertainty similar to that of the Victorians about the claims that art could appropriately make for itself. Paradoxically, both the antididacticism and the social philosophy of Modernist poetry express similar desires. The poetics which envisions a unified sensibility reflects a nostalgia both for significances to reveal themselves and for a lost psychological unity. That same nostalgia for universally apparent significance and for lost unity creates what at first seems a contradictory pressure toward didacticism. In ways similar to those of Arnold, Ruskin, Carlyle, or Tennyson, Yeats, Pound, and Eliot each desires a unified culture in which art, politics, and religion symbolically articulate a common system of belief. That desire pushes each of them toward the increasingly didactic exposition of cultural values in their poetry that has been identified with fascism. Both the radical experimentation with symbolist techniques and the conservative didacticism that characterizes Modernist poetry reflect a desire for a lost unity. Much as Arnold recommended, Modernist poets use the resources of poetry to create the lost cultural unity necessary to the psychological wholeness their earlier poetics envisions. Their attacks on Victorian didacticism, much like their attacks on Victorian rhetoric, express anger at the failure to attain the unified sensibility they desire. In their own turn toward the discursive definition of unified culture in their poetry, they paradoxically follow the pattern the Victorians had followed before them.

The idea of Victorianism, then, provides the Modernists with a way of historically polarizing a conflict to which the goals of their own poetics ultimately lead them. They identify Victorian poetry with the didactic pressure which operates ultimately on them as well, while they identify Modernism with the ideal of the unified sensibility which we have seen as an important element of Victorian poetics. This historical polarization leads them to simplify much Victorian poetry, and, with the exception of Yeats, to misrepresent Pater's achievement. Throughout his career, Yeats acknowledges Pater's importance, but Pound rarely mentions him, and Eliot aggressively belittles him, claiming that Pater had not influenced "a single first-rate mind of a later generation."[24] Although Victorian poetics contains many of the elements from which the Modernists were to build their poetic revolution, the Modernists characteristically misread Victorian poetry, identifying it with the failures which would most defeat their own enterprise.

The question of misreading brings us to the theories of influence constructed by Walter Jackson Bate and Harold Bloom. In *The Burden of the Past and the English Poet*, Bate argues that "the remorseless deepening of self-consciousness, before the rich and intimidating legacy of the past, has become the greatest single problem that modern art (art, that is to say, since the later seventeenth century) has had to face." He quotes T. S. Eliot, " 'Not only every great poet, but every genuine, though lesser poet, fulfills once for all some possibility of the language, and so leaves one possibility less for his successors.' " Bate continues, "Whatever he may say, or not say, about his predecessors, the poet from Dryden to Eliot has been unavoidably aware of them, and never so much as when he has tried to establish a difference."[25]

Bate argues that the poets of the eighteenth century surmounted the overpowering legacy of the Renaissance by a return to classical models which offered the advantage both of sufficient distance so as not to intimidate and of a superior claim to correctness. Bate's argument about the eighteenth century provides an insight about the Modernists because the way in which the Modernists reconstruct literary history shows a similar pattern. Each of them seeks to discredit the immediate past and erect some more distant model of literary value—the Chinese, the troubadours, Irish folk poetry, the metaphysicals. The very distance of the older poetry frees the poet from the intimidation closer models impose. And he can claim for each of them a cultural and psychological integration superior to his own immediate history.

Such models offer a further advantage as well. The Romantics imposed upon themselves and their successors the burden of originality. In assimilating poetics to the rhetoric of revolution and in making personal authenticity the test of value for poetry, they encouraged the sacrifice of the comforts tradition could offer. In their construction of individual literary histories, Yeats, Pound, and Eliot all attempt to regain the advantages of a traditional literary culture while claiming a peculiar originality as well, thus mediating between the pressure toward originality and the advantages of a tradition. Yeats writes, "Talk to me of originality and I will turn on you with rage."[26] In his discovery and creation of an Irish folk tradition to which he could assimilate his poetry, he attempts to achieve the commonality and public voice he desired and to free himself of the burden of originality. Yet the poet must discover, remake the tradition he owns, and in the very act of discovery of tradition achieve a claim to a special originality as well.

Yeats's discovery of a national identity allows him a simpler resolution of the tension between originality and tradition than either Eliot or Pound could attain, for they each attempt to transcend their American identity in attaching themselves to an international tradition. This international tradition, they separately argue, infuses new life into a decadent English poetry struggling under the destructive influence of Milton and the failures of the nineteenth century. In their construction of a literary tradition and in their placement of their own achievement within it, Eliot and Pound each mediates between tradition and originality. Eliot is highly conscious of this mediation both in "Tradition and the Individual Talent" and elsewhere. His diction frequently suggests that his construction of a concept of tradition enables him to come to terms with his poetic dependence upon the past. In "Tradition and the Individual Talent," Eliot writes that the individual poet will be aware

> that he must inevitably be judged by the standards of the past. I say judged, not amputated, by them; not judged to be as good as, or worse or better than, the dead; and certainly not judged by the canons of dead critics. It is a judgment, a comparison, in which two things are measured by each other. To conform merely would be for the new work not really to conform at all; it would not be new, and would therefore not be a work of art. And we do not quite say that the new is more valuable because it fits in; but its fitting in is a test of its value—a test, it is true, which can only be slowly and cautiously applied, for we are none of us infallible judges of conformity. We say: it appears to conform, and is perhaps individual, or it appears individual, and may conform; but we are hardly likely to find that it is one and not the other.[27]

By mediating between tradition and the individual talent, by owning a tradition he can possess, the poet assures he will be judged, not "amputated," and thus he maintains his individual identity. Eliot speaks elsewhere in similar terms. In "The Function of Criticism," he writes: "There is accordingly something outside of the artist to which he owes allegiance, a devotion to which he must surrender and sacrifice himself in order to earn and to obtain his unique position."[28] The artist achieves his unique position by "surrender" and "sacrifice" to tradition. In such a construction of the individual's relationship to history, Eliot has not sacrificed his claim to originality, as has been argued,[29] but has earned it in a unique way by claiming that self-historicization will save him from the burden of prior history. He at once achieves the advantages of tradition and a peculiar claim to historical significance.

Pound achieves this fusion in a different way by assimilating the history of literature to the model of science. He talks about inventors, who discover a particular process, and masters, who assimilate and coordinate a large number of preceding inventions. He composes his tradition of "the authors who actually invented something, or who are the 'first known examples' of the process in working order."[30] Much like Eliot's conception of tradition, Pound's construction of literary history according to a scientific model enables him to come to terms with his dependence on the past. Science offers a model of progress in which the future both builds and advances upon the achievements of the past. One never need ask the question "What is there left for me to do?" The discovery of new facts, of new techniques, the correction of the past permits the scientist new work. Pound's assimilation of literary history into the history of scientific discovery thus frees him from the anxiety that the best has been done, that there is nothing left to do. It also guarantees his own achievement. He can use the past and lay claim to his own invention.

In the literary traditions they all construct, however, Yeats, Eliot, and Pound in various ways and to various degrees belittle the Victorians and make themselves the authentic renovators of a decadent tradition. In the tradition he constructs in "How to Read," Pound asserts that British literature "was kept alive during the last century by a series of exotic injections." He excepts Browning from his general condemnation, but asserts his "grave limitations." After disposing of his predecessors, Pound makes the following claim: "All the developments in English verse since 1910 are due almost wholly to Americans. In fact, there is no longer any reason to call it English verse, and there is no present reason to think of England at all."[31] Pound thus secures his own claim to a place in the tradition. Yeats hails the defeat of Victorianism and makes a claim to advance upon even his admired predecessors in rediscovering "by our reintegration of the mind, our more profound Pre-Raphaelitism."[32] In explaining his own intention to reunify sensibility and to keep poetry distinct from those branches of thought with which it has nothing to do, Eliot criticizes the dissociated sensibility of the Victorians and their "various blundering attempts" to make alliances between various branches of thought.[33]

In belittling Victorian achievements and in presenting themselves as the saviors of a decadent tradition, modern poets are involved in the creative misreading that Harold Bloom has claimed dominates the history of poetry in the nineteenth and twentieth centuries. In *The Anxiety of Influence,* Bloom states his argument in the following way:

> Poetic Influence—when it involves two strong, authentic poets,—always proceeds by a misreading of the prior poet, an act of creative correction that is actually and necessarily a misinterpretation. The history of fruitful poetic influence, which is to say the main tradition of Western poetry since the Renaissance, is a history of anxiety and self-saving caricature, of distortion, of perverse, wilful revisionism without which modern poetry as such could not exist.[34]

Bloom's thesis offers one explanation of the belittlement with which the moderns frequently treat the Victorians and of their assertion that their own poetry makes a radical break with that of the past. The poets' critical writings offer some evidence that supports Bloom's thesis. In his *Autobiography,* Yeats makes a comment about Oscar Wilde which suggests some awareness of the process Bloom describes. Yeats writes that he would defend Wilde by saying that

> his very admiration for his predecessors in poetry, for Browning, for Swinburne and Rossetti, in their first vogue while he was a very young man, made any success seem impossible that could satisfy his immense ambition; never but once before had the artist seemed so great, never had the work of art seemed so difficult. I would then compare him with Benvenuto Cellini who, coming after Michael Angelo, found nothing left to do so satisfactory as to turn bravo and quarrel with the man who broke Michael Angelo's nose.[35]

Yeats's comment about Wilde suggests that he understands the destructive influence of admiration. His own criticism of the Victorians and his wary avoidance of the subject of Browning (in a letter he calls him "a dangerous influence") save him from that danger.[36]

Eliot too scarcely mentions Browning. The spectre of Arnold haunts his early prose, and he wages a running battle with him for critical preeminence.[37] He doesn't write his essay on Tennyson until 1936, and he then criticizes Tennyson for the very things one might criticize in Eliot himself—his constitutional melancholy, his difficulty with dramatic action, his abandonment of his finest poetic instincts for social orthodoxy. Eliot writes about Pater at considerable length while denigrating his achievement. After talking about *Marius the Epicurean* in some detail, Eliot makes the following abrupt and confusing turn: "I have spoken of the book as of some importance. I do not mean that its importance is due to any influence it may have exerted. I do not believe that Pater, in this book, has influenced a single first-rate mind of a later generation."[38]

For all of Pound's criticism of Victorian poetry and his credit to Browning, he has remarkably little to say about either. He uses Victorianism as a synonym for what he most dislikes.

> I reverence Dante and Villon and Catullus; for Milton and Victorianism and for the softness of the 'nineties' I have different degrees of antipathy or even contempt.

> Any natural wording, anything which keeps the mind off theatricals and on Klutaimnestra actual, dealing with an actual situation, and not pestering the reader with frills and festoons of language, is worth all the convoluted tushery that the Victorians can heap together.[39]

A passage in "Notes on Elizabethan Classicists" suggests the utility of the attitude.

> Only the mediocrity of a given time can drive the more intelligent men of that time to 'break with tradition.'
> I take it that the phrase 'break with tradition' is currently used to mean 'desert the more obvious imbecilities of one's immediate elders.'[40]

The passages that I have quoted show that Yeats, Pound, and Eliot each make statements and omissions that could justify Bloom's theory, according to which the Victorians had a powerful influence upon the Modernists that had to be overthrown by creative caricature. Such a theory seems to explain some relationships—that of Eliot to Arnold and to Pater, that of Pound to Browning—and it offers a fascinating model by which to read poems which reflect Eliot's swerve from Tennyson, for example, or Pound's from Browning. Nonetheless, it finally fails to offer a sufficient explanation for the process of historical distortion that we find in the idea of Victorianism. By encouraging us to see every distortion of the past as a creative caricature of a strong poet, Bloom's model simplifies the motives for historical distancing. The Modernists caricature the Victorians as much for their weaknesses as for their strengths. Each of the poets with whom I am dealing associates the Victorians with the failure he most fears for himself. For Yeats the Victorians are too passive, for Eliot they are too dissociated, and for Pound they are too diffuse. Each criticizes the Victorians for a lack of success in achieving the synthesis that he imagines as his own achievement. Creative caricature allows them not merely to overthrow an influence but to project a fear of failure on a discarded and alien past.

In addition to simplifying the motives for misreading, Bloom's model also encourages us to ignore the historical specificity of the problem. By using the family romance as a paradigm for literary influence, Bloom makes an author's peculiar relationship to his predecessors both personal and archetypal while he gives no place to its historical character as a modern phenomenon. Yet the model itself indicates the historical significance of the attitude toward the past that Bloom describes. In using the family romance to construct an idea of influence as an anxiety-creating, potentially paralyzing force, Bloom expresses a historically specific notion of the family as a crippling burden from which one struggles to free oneself. One reaches maturity by realizing one's difference, one's otherness, one's alienation, much as the writer can do his best work only when he has created his difference from his predecessors. Bloom has such success in using a modern idea of the family to represent a modern idea of literary influence because both alike reflect a changed sense of social identification. Modern man expresses his alienation by historicizing social relationships. Much as the caricature of the family in modern literature expresses a present social alienation by distorting and dismissing the past, so caricature of the literary past can express the alienation from his society that the writer specifically feels. From the latter part of the eighteenth century with the change in the patronage system and the conditions of publication, writers have felt increasingly unsure of their relationship to their audience. Moreover, the challenge to art's value offered by both science and utilitarianism made artists uncertain of what claim to an audience they possessed. Victorian literature everywhere reflects this uncertainty about art's ideological and social role. Modern poets share this uncertainty, but deal with it in part by historicizing it. Blundering attempts at syntheses, a facile social orthodoxy, the importation of ideological impurities are seen as a Victorian, not a modern, problem. The idea of Victorianism allows them to make the pressures under which they labor into a past which can be overthrown. The contempt that the moderns bestow on the Victorians measures their own discomfort with art's social and ideological role, but the act of separating past from present, Victorian from modern, offers a possibility of escape.

The way in which the terms "Victorian" and "modern" have been defined supports the idea that "Victorianism" provides a way of separating past from present. The word "Victorian" first seems to have been used to describe a literary period by the poet and critic Edmund Clarence Stedman, who published *Victorian Poets* in 1876. In his book Stedman argues that the Victorian period, a period characterized by "reflection, taste, repose," dominated by the influence of Tennyson and his idyllic method, was drawing to a close. New poets inspired by the example of Browning—Buchanan, Rossetti, Morris, and Swinburne—were struggling to break the restrictions that surrounded them in order "to reunite beauty and passion."[41] One might say that neither Queen Victoria nor Tennyson had the grace to die at the historically appropriate moment to fulfill Stedman's prophecy. Nonetheless, his use of "Victorian" to describe what he sees as an outmoded and restrictive literary style which has failed to meet the challenges that confront it shows that the word from the beginning of its use as a literary historical term carried pejorative connotations, describing a literature that was past, inadequate, ready to yield to a modern departure. The word "modern," on the other hand, is a very different kind of period designation, for it has no specific historical location. The word itself means characteristic of the present as opposed to the past. It implies at least a contrastive, if not a hostile, relationship to history. Indeed, Paul de Man has argued that modernity is characterized by the desire to forget the past, to originate something wholly new, however impossible to realize that desire may be.[42] The term itself is a paradoxical designation for a past literary period, a fact which has led to the increasing use of the term "Modernist" to describe that group of early twentieth-century writers who committed themselves to the modern. Furthermore, the way in which "modern" implies a present which displaces a past while "Victorian" describes a discarded past reveals much about the relationship of the two periods as constructions in literary history. Although they seem serial terms of historical description—after the Victorian period came the modern—they are frequently oppositional—the modern defeats, displaces, overcomes the Victorian.

The fact that terms which seem sequential historical descriptions are in fact interpretations constructed to defend a given point of view should surprise no historian. In his later prose T. S. Eliot admitted as much in asserting that his early criticism was a way of defending the kind of poetry that he wanted to write.[43] One way of making it new, as Pound desired, was to create a caricature of the immediate past which could then be enlisted to prove one's claim to modernity. In "Second Thoughts on Literary Periods," Claudio Guillen observes that no system of norms, standards, or conventions is merely given to us, that a complex of this kind proceeds from the questions we choose to direct to single works.[44] The questions which have resulted in the complex we call Victorianism seem designed to prove the success of Modernism, to emphasize the qualities which distance and dissociate the literature of the previous period from our most prestigious twentieth-century literature. Much as the Victorians created a simplified conception of Romanticism to fulfill the needs of their own poetics, so the Modernists constructed an idea of Victorianism in order to make claims about their own poetry. We sympathize with the freedom that poets take in creating a climate congenial for their work, but we should nonetheless be wary of accepting the past that they construct as a historical description.

Guillen argues that literary historians are particularly liable to the error of static interpretations of history. We tend to see individual literary works as occupying a timeless ideal realm. Indeed, works often claim this status for themselves. When we group literary works according to their time of composition to develop the interpretation called a period, the pressure toward the ideal that is so much a part of our reading of the individual work encourages us to construct broad and stationary patterns of periodization. The literary historian may thus develop broad generalizations about the series of works associated with a given period without ever considering the movement and flux of history. Thus categories which seem historical can in fact rationalize historical development in a series of ahistorical constructions.[45] Because of the way in which "Victorian" and "modern" have been used as rhetorical opposites, they offer a particularly acute example of the phenomenon Guillen describes. Relying upon Modernist interpretations of Victorianism blinds us to the complex affinities in the literature written from 1830 to 1930. The Modernists themselves had a vested interest in denying these affinities. Not only did they threaten their claim to the modern, but they undermined Modernist poetics at the point of their greatest similarity to those of the nineteenth century and at the point of greatest vulnerability. That literature present the object as in itself it really is, that it escape the burden of personality, was a desire that Victorian and modern poets shared. The very difficulties of realizing such a desire encourage a break with history, a history which exposes the limits under which we labor.

Notes

Chapter 1

1. Ezra Pound, "A Retrospect," *Literary Essays,* ed. T. S. Eliot (New York: New Directions, 1968), p. 11.

2. T. S. Eliot, "The Metaphysical Poets," *Selected Essays* (New York: Harcourt, Brace and World, 1964), p. 248.

3. W. B. Yeats, "Modern Poetry," *Essays and Introductions* (New York: Collier Books, 1973), p. 495.

4. Cleanth Brooks, *Modern Poetry and the Tradition* (New York: Oxford University Press, 1965), p. 239.

5. Ibid., p. xiv.

6. See Frank Kermode, *Romantic Image* (New York: Vintage Books, 1964); Robert Langbaum, *The Poetry of Experience: The Dramatic Monologue in Modern Literary Tradition* (New York: W. W. Norton, 1963); Harold Bloom, *Yeats* (New York: Oxford University Press, 1970), and *The Ringers in the Tower: Studies in Romantic Tradition* (Chicago: University of Chicago Press, 1971); George Bornstein, *Transformations of Romanticism in Yeats, Eliot, and Stevens* (Chicago: University of Chicago Press, 1976). In "From Victorian to Modern: A Sketch for a Critical Reappraisal," *The Victorian Newsletter* 32 (Fall 1967):20–28, Norman Friedman argues that Victorian poetics contains Modernistic attitudes toward art's truth whose ultimate source is Romanticism. Richard Fallis and Charles Altieri both have written essays which directly confront the relationship of Victorianism to Modernism: Richard Fallis, "Yeats and the Reinterpretation of Victorian Poetry," *Victorian Poetry* 14 (1976):89–100; Charles Altieri, "Arnold and Tennyson: The Plight of Victorian Lyricism as Context of Modernism," *Criticism* 20 (1978): 281–306. Both essays take as their starting point Modernist criticism of Victorian poetry, then offer detailed illustrations of these criticisms, taking for granted Modernism's success in overcoming the dissociations they describe. Such arguments fail to examine the rhetorical purpose of Modernist criticisms of Victorian poetry and exempt Modernism from the historical scrutiny that they give to the Victorians. They thus repeat Brooks's argument (which is Eliot's and Yeats's argument) in a more sophisticated form.

7. Matthew Arnold, "Preface to the First Edition of *Poems*," *The Poems of Matthew Arnold*, ed. Kenneth Allott (New York: Barnes and Noble, 1965), p. 599.

8. In *Transformations of Romanticism in Yeats, Eliot, and Stevens*, George Bornstein makes this definition of the continuity of nineteenth- and twentieth-century poetry (pp. 1–26).

9. M. H. Abrams, *The Mirror and the Lamp: Romantic Theory and the Critical Tradition* (New York: W. W. Norton, 1958), pp. 47–69.

10. See particularly Paul De Man, "Intentional Structure of the Romantic Nature Image," in *Romanticism and Consciousness*, ed. Harold Bloom (New York: W. W. Norton, 1970), pp. 65–77.

11. Thomas Carlyle, *Sartor Resartus*, in *The Works of Thomas Carlyle* (New York: Charles Scribner's Sons, 1899–1901), 1:153.

12. Arnold, "Preface," pp. 598–99.

13. Ibid., p. 591.

14. Ibid., p. 593.

15. Robert Browning, *Pauline*, ed. N. Hardy Wallis (London: University of London Press, 1931), 11. 937–39 (1833 text).

16. For a recent study of Tennyson's relationship to the Romantic tradition, see Margaret A. Lourie, "Tennyson as Romantic Revisionist," *Studies in Romanticism* 18 (1979):3–27.

17. For a study of this attempt, see Zelda Boyd, "What the Poet Sees: A Study of the Aesthetic Theories of Mill, Carlyle, Ruskin, and Arnold" (Ph.D. diss., University of Michigan, 1971).

18. Matthew Arnold, "The Function of Criticism at the Present Time," *Lectures and Essays in Criticism*, ed. R. H. Super (Ann Arbor: University of Michigan Press, 1973), p. 258.

19. Matthew Arnold, "Wordsworth," *English Literature and Irish Politics*, ed. R. H. Super (Ann Arbor: University of Michigan Press, 1973), p. 52.

20. Matthew Arnold, "Bryon," *English Literature and Irish Politics*, p. 234.

21. Arnold, "Wordsworth," p. 53.

22. T. S. Eliot, *The Sacred Wood* (London: Methuen, 1960), pp. 31–32.

23. Ibid., pp. xi–xii.

24. Ibid., pp. 157–58.

25. T. S. Eliot, "The Function of Criticism," *Selected Essays*, p. 15. For an excellent discussion of the psychological function of Eliot's anti-Romanticism, see George Bornstein, *Transformations of Romanticism in Yeats, Eliot, and Stevens*, pp. 94–162.

26. See Ronald Schuchard, "T. S. Eliot as an Extension Lecturer, 1916–1919," *Review of English Studies* ns 25 (1974):165.

27. See particularly his definition of the perfect critic in *The Sacred Wood*, p. 15.

28. T. S. Eliot, "The Function of Criticism," *Selected Essays*, p. 16.

29. For an account of Pound's heterodox view of the Romantics, see Hugh Witemeyer, "Walter Savage Landor and Ezra Pound," *Romantic and Modern: Evaluations of a Literary Tradition*, ed. George Bornstein (Pittsburgh: University of Pittsburgh Press, 1977), pp. 147–63. See also George Bornstein's account of Pound as a critic of Romanticism in *The Postromantic Consciousness of Ezra Pound*, English Literary Studies Monograph Series, no. 8 (Victoria, B.C.: University of Victoria, 1977), pp. 19–34.

30. Ezra Pound, "The Rev. G. Crabbe, LL.B.," *Literary Essays*, p. 276.

31. Ibid., p. 277.

32. W. B. Yeats, "William Blake and the Imagination," *Essays and Introductions*, p. 114.

33. W. B. Yeats, "Prometheus Unbound," *Essays and Introductions*, pp. 421–22.

34. W. B. Yeats, "A General Introduction for My Work," *Essays and Introductions*, p. 509.

35. In *Syntax in English Poetry: 1870–1930* (Berkeley: University of California Press, 1967), for example, William E. Baker describes continuities between Victorian and modern poetic style in which the elaborately periodic structure of Browning, Swinburne, and Hopkins anticipates the more radical fragmentation of modern poetry.

Chapter 2

1. Randall Jarrell, *Poetry and the Age* (New York: Alfred A. Knopf, 1953), p. 13.

2. See Robert Langbaum, *The Poetry of Experience: The Dramatic Monologue in Modern Literary Tradition;* Philip Hobsbaum, "The Rise of the Dramatic Monologue," *Hudson Review* 28 (1975):227–45; Alan Sinfield, *Dramatic Monologue* (London: Methuen, 1977).

3. Ezra Pound, "T. S. Eliot," *Literary Essays*, pp. 219–40.

4. T. S. Eliot, "The Method of Mr. Pound," *Athenaeum*, 24 October 1919.

5. W. B. Yeats, *The Autobiography of William Butler Yeats* (New York: Macmillan, 1974), pp. 88, 317–18. See also George Russell's comment that Yeats vigorously defended Wilde "against the charge of being a poseur. He said it was merely living artistically, and it was the duty of everybody to conceive of himself." Quoted by Richard Ellmann in *Yeats: The Man and the Masks* (New York: E. P. Dutton, 1948), p. 74.

In *Eminent Domain* (New York: Oxford University Press, 1967), pp. 9–27, Richard Ellmann argues the influence of Wilde upon Yeats in his development of the idea of the mask.

6. Oscar Wilde, "The Critic as Artist," *The Works of Oscar Wilde* (New York: Lamb Publishing Co., 1909), 10:116.

7. Ezra Pound, "Chinese Poetry—II," *Today* 3 (1918):93; Hobsbaum, "Rise of Dramatic Monologue"; A. Dwight Culler, "Monodrama and the Dramatic Monologue," *PMLA* 90 (1975):366–85.

8. Ralph Rader, "The Dramatic Monologue and Related Lyric Forms," *Critical Inquiry* 3 (1976):131–51.

9. J. S. Mill, *Essays on Poetry*, ed. F. Parvin Sharpless (Columbia: University of South Carolina Press, 1976), p. 26.

10. All quotations from Browning's poetry in my text are from *The Complete Poetic and Dramatic Works of Robert Browning* (Boston: Houghton Mifflin, 1895).

11. Browning made the remark both in a note to an edition of *Pauline* published in 1868 and in an advertisement to *Dramatic Lyrics* published in 1852.

12. Langbaum, *The Poetry of Experience*, p. 157.

13. Robert Browning, "An Essay on Shelley," *The Complete Poetic and Dramatic Works*, pp. 1009, 1008.

14. In *The Disappearance of God* (Cambridge: Harvard University Press, 1963), J. Hillis Miller uses a similar tension to define Browning's attitude toward God.

15. Culler, "Monodrama and the Dramatic Monologue."

16. T. S. Eliot, *"In Memoriam," Selected Essays,* p. 289.

17. Although Matthew Arnold wrote very few dramatic monologues, he shows a continuing concern with the same problems which I have argued motivate Browning's and Tennyson's development of the dramatic monologue. Like Browning and Tennyson, he both feared the self-imprisonment which self-consciousness imposed and sought ways to objectify poetic emotion. I will treat Arnold's attempts to find objective bases for poetic emotion in later chapters.

18. Hobsbaum gives a useful description of the later imitators of Browning. He further argues that Pound was influenced by Browning's followers ("The Rise of the Dramatic Monologue," pp. 241–42).

19. See Patricia Ball, *The Central Self: A Study in Romantic and Victorian Imagination* (London: Athlone Press, 1968), and E. D. H. Johnson, *The Alien Vision of Victorian Poetry* (Princeton: Princeton University Press, 1952), for discussion of the Victorian consciousness of this problem. In *W. B. Yeats: The Later Poetry* (Berkeley: University of California Press, 1971), pp. 1–72, Thomas Parkinson writes of the modern consciousness of the problem; and in *The Situation of Poetry: Contemporary Poetry and Its Traditions* (Princeton: Princeton University Press, 1976), Robert Pinsky discusses the impact of the problem on contemporary poetry.

20. Walter Pater, *The Renaissance,* (London: Macmillan, 1900), p. 235.

21. Ibid., p. 238.

22. Wilde, "The Critic as Artist," p. 210.

23. Most critics who treat the modern use of persona emphasize its resolution rather than its sustaining of conflict. In the major study of modernist uses of persona, *The Poet in the Poem: The Personae of Eliot, Yeats, and Pound* (Berkeley: University of California Press, 1960), George T. Wright argues that the device of persona enables the modern poet to shift our attention from the self as the center of reality to a total vision embodied in the permanence of poetic form. In the chapter of her book *Browning and the Modern Tradition* (London: Macmillan, 1976), concerned with the dramatic method, Betty S. Flowers's emphasis is more technical. She argues that modern poets find a greater freedom of poetic form in developing Browning's fusion of dramatic and lyric techniques. In *Dramatic Monologue,* Alan Sinfield stresses the centrality of the "feint" to the dramatic monologue, the instability of the relationship between the voice of the poet and his persona. He argues that Modernist poets exploit this instability more than their Victorian predecessors, but he concludes that the dramatic monologue constitutes a provisional language whereby the poet ultimately develops a first-person voice which does not suffer the disadvantages of the Romantic "I" which the Victorians sought to avoid.

24. Yeats, *The Autobiography,* pp. 68–69.

25. Yeats, "A General Introduction for My Work," *Essays and Introductions,* pp. 510–11.

26. Yeats, *The Autobiography,* p. 102.

27. Richard Ellmann, *Yeats: The Man and the Masks,* p. 171, and *The Identity of Yeats* (New York: Oxford University Press, 1954), p. 93.

28. Yeats, *The Autobiography,* p. 311.

29. Ibid., p. 102.

30. Ibid., p. 128.

31. Robert Laugbaum, *The Mysteries of Identity* (New York: Oxford University Press, 1977), pp. 159–69.

32. See Ellmann, *Yeats: The Man and the Masks* and *The Identity of Yeats*.

33. A note in which Yeats explains his use of characters from "The Secret Rose" suggests that even his attachment of poems to legendary figures reflects an effort to embody psychological principles rather than actual characters. He asserts of the speakers of the poems in *The Wind Among the Reeds*, "I have used them in this book more as principles of the mind than as actual personages." *The Variorum Edition of the Poems of W. B. Yeats*, ed. Peter Allt and Russell K. Alspach (New York: Macmillan, 1965), p. 803.

34. I am indebted to Thomas Parkinson's *W. B. Yeats: The Later Poetry* for its delineation of the differing modes Yeats combines in constructing the lyric of multiple voice. In *The Poet in the Poem*, Wright builds upon Parkinson's analysis to argue that Yeats moves from an idealized persona in the early poems to a persona in the later poems portrayed in its circumstantial location, with its weaknesses as well as its strengths, grasping toward an ideal. Yeats's progress, as Wright defines it, illustrates a paradox in Yeats's development of the concept of mask. The strain upon the self to be poetical required by a poetics of sincerity results in a far more artificial persona than the multiplicity and artifice cultivated in the concept of mask.

35. W. B. Yeats, *Mythologies* (London: Macmillan, 1959), p. 329.

36. Bloom, *Yeats*, p. 329.

37. Quoted by Ellmann in *The Identity of Yeats*, pp. 239–40.

38. Ezra Pound, "Arnold Dolmetsch," *Literary Essays*, p. 431. Compare this passage from Pound's *The Spirit of Romance* (Norfolk, Conn.: New Directions, 1952), p. 92: "I believe that Greek myth arose when someone having passed through delightful psychic experience tried to communicate it to others and found it necessary to screen himself from persecution."

39. Ezra Pound, *A Lume Spento and Other Early Poems* (New York: New Directions, 1965), p. 52.

40. Donald Davie, *Ezra Pound: Poet as Sculptor* (New York: Oxford University Press, 1964), pp. 82–83.

41. Pound, "T. S. Eliot," *Literary Essays*, pp. 419–20.

42. *The Letters of Ezra Pound, 1907–1941*, ed. D. D. Paige (London: Faber and Faber, 1951), p. 294.

43. See, for example, Davie, *Ezra Pound*, p. 23; Herbert N. Schneidau, *Ezra Pound: The Image and the Real* (Baton Rouge: Louisiana State University Press, 1969), pp. 163–67; N. Christoph de Nagy, "Pound and Browning," in *New Approaches to Ezra Pound*, ed. Eva Hesse (Berkeley: University of California Press, 1969), pp. 86–124. Hugh Witemeyer's argument in *The Poetry of Ezra Pound: Forms and Renewal, 1908–1920* (Berkeley: University of California Press, 1969) provides an exception in its emphasis on the provisional identities and the historical verisimilitude that personae afforded both Browning and Pound (pp. 60–87).

44. *Robert Browning and Julia Wedgewood: A Broken Friendship as Revealed by Their Letters*, ed. Richard Curle (New York: Frederick A. Stokes, 1937), p. 29. In *The Early Poetry of Ezra Pound* (Cambridge: Harvard University Press, 1968), pp. 3–60, Thomas H. Jackson argues that Pound departs from the influence of

Browning in the stress he places upon the idea of the moment. Jackson then proceeds to locate the idea of the moment as an influence upon Pound in the poetry of the Pre-Raphaelites and the Decadents. I do not want to deny Pre-Raphaelite influence upon Pound; I see the idea of the moment as central to Browning's poetics, as I argue in *The Finer Optic: The Aesthetic of Particularity in Victorian Poetry* (New Haven: Yale University Press, 1975), pp. 111–25.

45. Pound, *Letters*, p. 36.

46. Ezra Pound, *Gaudier-Brzeska* (New York: New Directions, 1970), p. 85.

47. In *The Poet in the Poem*, p. 144, George Wright argues that Pound gives increasing objectivity to the mask as an "impersonal" formal correlative of the poet's emotion. This reading of Pound's career does not allow him to make sense of *Hugh Selwyn Mauberley*, which he dismisses as a failure (p. 148).

48. The inability of critics to reach any general agreement about who speaks which poems or about how well Pound controls his persona illustrates this difficulty. Frustrated by Pound's seeming inconsistency, some critics have argued the irrelevancy of understanding Mauberley as a character. Davie dismisses the Mauberley persona as "a distracting nuisance" (p. 101). In *Ezra Pound: The Image and the Real*, pp. 163–72, Herbert Schneidau argues that Mauberley exists not as a character but as a set of momentary inflections or Jamesian reflectors with which Pound conveys a series of events. I feel that our uneasiness about the boundaries of the character is very much to the point in reading the poem. Sinfield suggests a similar point when he observes that Pound refuses "to allow the reader to rest in any one interpretation of the status of the speaker" (p. 70).

49. Eliot, *"In Memoriam," Literary Essays*, p. 289.

50. Eliot, *Literary Essays*, p. 7.

51. Ibid., pp. 7, 8.

52. Ibid.

53. Ibid., pp. 10–11.

54. Ibid., p. 8.

55. See Hugh Kenner, *The Poetry of Ezra Pound* (London: Faber and Faber, 1951), pp. 119–25; Maynard Mack, "The Muse of Satire," *Yale Review* 41 (1951):80–92; William B. Ewald, *The Masks of Jonathan Swift* (New York: Russell and Russell, 1954), pp. 1–12; Rebecca Price Parkin, *The Poetic Workmanship of Alexander Pope* (Minneapolis: University of Minnesota Press, 1955), pp. 7–30. Robert C. Elliott's *The Literary Persona* (Chicago: University of Chicago Press, 1982) provides an excellent critical history of the concept of persona which argues in much the way I do about the relationship of persona as a critical term to Modernist poetics. Elliott locates the shift in assumption that poetry should not be confessional but impersonal at the beginning of the twentieth century. I locate that shift earlier in the Victorian preoccupation with the dramatic monologue, which anticipates the Modernist concern with persona and impersonality.

56. T. S. Eliot, *On Poetry and Poets* (New York: Noonday Press, 1961), pp. 103–4.

57. For a critical account of this incongruity, see Walter J. Ong, "The Jinee in the Well Wrought Urn," in *The Barbarian Within* (New York: Macmillan, 1954), pp. 15–25.

58. The Jamesian conception of point of view resembles the idea of persona in the way in which it contains a tension between subjective and objective. James's development of point of view at once recognizes the subjective nature of truth

while it strives to give that truth an objective existence in the work of art within which the author as a separate individual has no existence. Like persona, point of view acknowledges the determining role played by personal perspective while it seeks to detach the work of art from the personality of the author. The work at once embodies a limited subjective vision of reality while it transcends that vision in the status it claims for itself as a work of art. James supplies an important link between Victorian and modern uses of persona. He develops a conception of point of view implicit within the Victorian novel and dramatic monologue which influences both Eliot and Pound in their creation of personae. Pound wrote of *Hugh Selwyn Mauberley:* "(Of course, I'm no more Mauberley than Eliot is Prufrock. Mais passons.) Mauberley is a mere surface. Again a study in form, an attempt to condense the James novel. Meliora speramus." *Letters*, p. 180.

59. See Pinsky, pp. 13–16.

60. Helen Vendler makes this point in *On Extended Wings: Wallace Stevens' Longer Poems* (Cambridge: Harvard University Press, 1969), p. 68.

61. Donald Davie, "On Sincerity," *Encounter*, October 1968, p. 64.

Chapter 3

1. Yeats, "Modern Poetry," *Essays and Introductions*, p. 495.

2. Eliot, *Selected Essays*, p. 247.

3. Pound, "A Retrospect," *Literary Essays*, p. 11.

4. Yeats, "Modern Poetry," p. 495.

5. Eliot, *Selected Essays*, p. 246.

6. Pound, "A Retrospect," p. 4.

7. Arthur Hallam, "On Some of the Characteristics of Modern Poetry and on the Lyrical Poems of Alfred Tennyson," *The Writings of Arthur Hallam*, ed. T. H. Vail Motter (New York: MLA, 1943), pp. 182–98.

8. See particularly Isobel Armstrong's work in *Victorian Scrutinies: Reviews of Poetry, 1830–1870* (London: Athlone Press, 1972, and "The Role and Treatment of Emotion in Victorian Criticism of Poetry," *Victorian Periodicals Newsletter*, 10 (1977):3–16. Armstrong makes an argument similar to mine about the Hallam essay, but she feels that the attempt to find objective grounds for emotion separates Victorian from Modernist poetry.

9. W. B. Yeats, "A Bundle of Poets," *Uncollected Prose*, ed. John P. Frayne (New York: Columbia University Press, 1970), 1:277.

10. Yeats, "Art and Ideas," *Essays and Introductions*, p. 347.

11. Marshall McLuhan, "Tennyson and Picturesque Poetry," in *Critical Essays on the Poetry of Tennyson*, ed. John Killham (New York: Barnes and Noble, 1960), pp. 67–85.

12. Ezra Pound, *The Spirit of Romance*, p. 14.

13. F. N. Lees also notes the similarity of Hallam's analysis to Eliot's description of the dissociation of sensibility, in "The Dissociation of Sensibility: Arthur Hallam and T. S. Eliot," *Notes and Queries* 14 (1967):308–9.

14. Hallam, "On Some of the Characteristics of Modern Poetry," p. 190.

15. Kermode, *Romantic Image*, pp. 138–61.

16. Hallam, p. 187.

17. Ibid., p. 186.

18. Eliot, "The Metaphysical Poets," *Selected Essays*, pp. 246, 249.

19. Hallam, p. 187.

20. Ibid., pp. 191–92.

21. Armstrong, "The Role and Treatment of Emotion in Victorian Criticism of Poetry," p. 10.

22. Hallam, pp. 187–88.

23. Yeats, "Art and Ideas," *Essays and Introductions*, p. 348.

24. *The Letters of John Keats*, ed. Hyder Edward Rollins (Cambridge: Harvard University Press, 1958), 2:323.

25. Mill, "Tennyson's Poems," *Essays on Poetry*, p. 48.

26. A. Dwight Culler, *The Poetry of Tennyson* (New Haven: Yale University Press, 1977), p. 38.

27. Mill, "Tennyson's Poems," p. 70.

28. Hallam, "On Some of the Characteristics of Modern Poetry," pp. 194–95.

29. Culler, *The Poetry of Tennyson*, p. 4.

30. Boyd, "What the Poet Sees: A Study of the Aesthetic Theories of Mill, Carlyle, Ruskin, and Arnold," pp. 167–68.

31. Thomas Carlyle, *On Heroes, Hero-Worship, and the Heroic in History. The Works of Thomas Carlyle*, 1:105, 104, 108. Boyd discusses George Eliot's image of the pier-glass in *Middlemarch* (chap. 27) as an example of a similar concept of perception (pp. 13–14). In Eliot's image, a candle, like the egoism of any person informing perception of events, makes the disordered scratches on a mirror appear to arrange themselves in concentric circles.

32. Arnold, *The Poems of Matthew Arnold*, pp. 593–94.

33. John Ruskin, *Modern Painters, The Works of John Ruskin*, ed. E. T. Cook and Alexander Wedderburn (London: George Allen, 1904–12), 5:204, 210, 211.

34. Ibid., pp. 386–87.

35. Ibid., 3:331–32.

36. Ibid., p. 335.

37. Ibid., 5:387. See Patricia Ball, *The Science of Aspects* (London: Athone Press, 1971), for an analysis of the role of fact in Ruskin's criticism that supports my own (pp. 48–102). See also Boyd, "What the Poet Sees," p. 125, for an argument about Ruskin's "impressionism."

38. Pound, *Gaudier-Brzeska*, p. 89.

39. Bloom, *Yeats*, p. 106.

40. Ruskin, *Works*, 12:159.

41. All quotations from the poetry of Hopkins in my text are from *The Poems of Gerard Manley Hopkins*, ed. W. H. Gardner and N. H. MacKenzie (London: Oxford University Press, 1967).

42. Pound, *Gaudier-Brzeska*, p. 89.

43. Jacob Korg has written a stimulating essay on the linguistic consequences of this fear in "Hopkins' Linguistic Deviations," *PMLA* 92 (1977):977–86.

44. Pater, *The Renaissance*, p. x.

45. Ibid., p. xi.

46. Ibid., p. 53.

47. Ibid., p. xii.

48. Yeats, *The Autobiography*, p. 323.

49. Yeats, "Art and Ideas," *Essays and Introductions*, p. 347.

50. Yeats, *The Autobiography*, p. 201.

51. Yeats, "Art and Ideas," *Essays and Introductions*, p. 347.

52. Yeats, "The Symbolism of Poetry," *Essays and Introductions*, pp. 156–57.

53. Yeats, "Art and Ideas," *Essays and Introductions*, p. 348.

54. Yeats, "Modern Poetry," *Essays and Introductions*, p. 495. Yeats's criticism of Tennyson does in fact reflect Tennyson's development away from Hallam's principles. For an excellent discussion of Yeats's relationship to Tennyson, see George Bornstein, "Last Romantic or Last Victorian: Yeats, Tennyson, and Browning," *Yeats Annual, No. 1* (1982), pp. 114–32. Bornstein argues that Yeats creates a construction of Tennyson's career that expresses the dangers that he feared for his own poetry.

55. Yeats, "The Happiest of the Poets," *Essays and Introductions*, p. 53.

56. Yeats, *The Autobiography*, p. 201.

57. Yeats, "Art and Ideas," *Essays and Introductions*, p. 349.

58. W. B. Yeats, Introduction, *The Oxford Book of Modern Verse* (Oxford: Clarendon Press, 1936), p. xxvii.

59. Ibid., p. xxviii.

60. Ibid., p. xxx.

61. Yeats, *Essays and Introductions*, p. 271.

62. Ibid., p. 272.

63. Yeats, "The Happiest of the Poets," *Essays and Introductions*, p. 64.

64. Yeats, *The Autobiography*, p. 332.

65. Yeats, ibid., p. 127.

66. See Parkinson, *W. B. Yeats: The Later Poetry*.

67. Yeats, "Art and Ideas," *Essays and Introductions*, p. 349.

68. Ibid., pp. 353–54.

69. Ibid., p. 355.

70. Yeats, "Discoveries," *Essays and Introductions*, pp. 267–78.

71. Eliot, "Hamlet and His Problems," *Selected Essays*, p. 126.

72. Ibid., p. 125.

73. Eliot, "Dante," *Selected Essays*, p. 205.

74. Eliot, "Rudyard Kipling," *On Poetry and Poets*, p. 289.

75. Eliot, "Lancelot Andrewes," *Selected Essays*, pp. 308–09.

76. Eliot, "Reflections on Contemporary Poetry," *The Egoist*, Sept. 1917, p. 118.

77. Eliot, "Dante," *Selected Essays*, p. 204.

78. Eliot, "Rhetoric and Poetic Drama," *Selected Essays*, p. 29.

79. Eliot, "Philip Massinger," *Selected Essays*, p. 189.

80. Ibid., p. 187.

81. Ibid., p. 185.

82. Eliot, "Swinburne as Poet," *Selected Essays*, p. 285.

83. Ibid.

84. See Graham Hough, "The Poet as Critic," in *The Literary Criticism of T. S. Eliot*, ed. David Newton De-Molina (London: Athlone Press, 1977), pp. 42–63.

85. See Mowbray Allan, *T. S. Eliot's Impersonal Theory of Poetry* (Lewisburg: Bucknell University Press, 1974); Bornstein, *Transformations of Romanticism in Yeats, Eliot, and Stevens;* C. K. Stead, "Eliot, Arnold, and the English Poetic Tradition," in *The Literary Criticism of T. S. Eliot*, pp. 184–206; Edward Lobb, *T. S. Eliot and the Romantic Critical Tradition* (London: Routledge and Kegan Paul, 1981). Although Allan does not link Eliot to the Victorians in his description of Eliot's transformation of Romanticism, he also emphasizes Eliot's use of sensation and

seeing the object as it is to escape the subjectivism that he fears in the idealist epistemology of Romanticism.

86. Eliot, *The Sacred Wood*, p. 11.

87. Eliot, "Philip Massinger," *Selected Essays*, p. 181.

88. Eliot, *The Sacred Wood*, p. 15.

89. Eliot, "The Function of Criticism," *Selected Essays*, pp. 21–22.

90. Ibid., p. 20.

91. Ibid., p. 22.

92. In "The Aesthetic Moment in Landscape Poetry" (*The Interior Landscape: The Literary Criticism of Marshall McLuhan, 1943–1962*, ed. Eugene McNamara [New York: McGraw-Hill, 1969], pp. 157–67), Marshall McLuhan distinguishes between the aesthetic moment in Pre-Raphaelite poetry and in Modernist poetry in a way that supports the distinction and similarity that I am trying to draw. McLuhan argues that the Pre-Raphaelites used subject matter to achieve intensity, whereas the Modernists achieved intensity by splitting up the arrested moment of cognition into numerous fragments which could be orchestrated in discontinuous ways. Nonetheless, McLuhan states, landscape is an indispensable technique for managing the aesthetic moment in poetry.

93. Eliot, Preface to St. John Perse, *Anabase* (London: Faber and Faber, 1959), pp. 9–10.

94. Eliot, *On Poetry and Poets*, pp. 22–23.

95. Eliot, *The Sacred Wood*, p. 9.

96. Pound, *Gaudier-Brzeska*, pp. 85, 86.

97. Pound, "A Retrospect," *Literary Essays*, p. 3.

98. Pound, "Dubliners and Mr. James Joyce," *Literary Essays*, p. 399.

99. Pound, *Gaudier-Brzeska*, p. 89.

100. Ibid., p. 87.

101. Pound, *The Spirit of Romance*, p. 14.

102. Pound, *Gaudier-Brzeska*, p. 92.

103. Pound, "A Retrospect," *Literary Essays*, p. 5.

104. Davie, *Ezra Pound: Poet as Sculptor*, pp. 73–74.

105. In *Ezra Pound: The Image and the Real*, Herbert Schneidau quotes Davie's distinction, calls it unfair to Eliot, but applies it to Hulme (p. 66). Without minimizing the distinctions between Pound and Hulme, I would argue that an impressionist poetics such as Pound and Hulme share can motivate opposite attitudes toward language. On the one hand, one can assimilate words to things completely as Pound attempted to do, and so possess a boundless faith in language's power of nomination. On the other hand, impressionism can also lead to a sense of language as a synthetic counter as Hulme had. Both attitudes toward language result from the belief that poetry concerns a pure reality beyond language for which language is either a clear or a cloudy mirror.

106. Pound, *Gaudier-Brzeska*, p. 92.

107. Ernest Fenollosa, "The Chinese Written Character as a Medium for Poetry," *Instigations of Ezra Pound* (New York: Boni and Liveright, 1920), p. 362.

108. Ibid., pp. 362, 363.

109. Ibid., pp. 365–66.

110. Ibid., p. 377.

111. Schneidau, *Ezra Pound: The Image and the Real*, pp. 56–73. In "Pound and Fenollosa: The Problem of Influence," *Critical Quarterly* 20 (Spring 1978):48–60,

Loy Martin argues that Fenollosa's essay describes the syntactic characteristics of Victorian poetry in its reliance upon the relative clause to specify temporal orientation more accurately than Pound's effort to achieve spatial juxtaposition in which the object functions as emotional sign. Martin's argument makes telling distinctions while it also supports the link between Fenollosa, Pound, and Victorian poetics because they share an interest in the object as an emotional sign. This interest draws Pound to the Fenollosa essay, and it makes the Fenollosa essay an appropriate description of Victorian poetic practice.

112. Pound, "The Teacher's Mission," *Literary Essays*, p. 61.

113. Pound, "Early Translators of Homer," *Literary Essays*, p. 267.

114. Quoted by Thomas H. Jackson, *The Early Poetry of Ezra Pound*, p. 249.

115. Yeats, Introduction, *The Oxford Book of Modern Verse*, p. xxx.

116. Ibid., p. xxv.

117. L. S. Dembo, *Conceptions of Reality in Modern American Poetry* (Berkeley: University of California Press, 1966), pp. 6–7.

118. Jonathan Culler, "Literary History, Allegory, and Semiology," *New Literary History* 7 (1976):249–70.

Chapter 4

1. *Mill's Essays on Literature and Society*, ed. J. B. Schneewind (New York: Macmillan, 1965), p. 28.

2. See Karl Mannheim, "Historicism," *Essays on the Sociology of Knowledge* (London: Routledge and Kegan Paul, 1952), pp. 84–85. For the ways in which historicism dominates nineteenth-century thought and literature, see Maurice Mandelbaum, *History, Man, and Reason* (Baltimore: Johns Hopkins University Press, 1971).

3. For discussion of the impact of nineteenth-century thinking on Victorian poetry, see Jerome Buckley, *The Triumph of Time: A Study of the Victorian Concepts of Time, History, Progress, and Decadence* (Cambridge: Belknap Press, 1966); Gerald L. Bruns, "The Formal Nature of Victorian Thinking," *PMLA* 90 (1965):904–18; and Peter Allan Dale, *The Victorian Critic and the Idea of History* (Cambridge: Harvard University Press, 1977).

4. In arguing that Victorian literature shows a conflict between transcendent and historical modes of thought, I disagree with Bruns's analysis in "The Formal Nature of Victorian Thinking," where he argues that Victorian writers overcome the conflict between process and absolute, successfully transforming transcendent categories of thought into historical ones.

5. For an essay on Arnold's peculiarly modern distress over history, see David J. DeLaura, "Matthew Arnold and the Nightmare of History," in *Victorian Poetry*, Stratford-Upon-Avon Studies, 15 (London: Edward Arnold, 1972), pp. 37–57.

6. Arnold, "Stanzas from the Grande Chartreuse" (11. 85–86), *Poems*.

7. "Preface to the First Edition of *Poems*" (1853), pp. 593–94.

8. *The Correspondence of Arthur Hugh Clough*, ed. Frederick L. Mulhauser (Oxford: Clarendon Press, 1957), ii, 546.

9. *Letters of Matthew Arnold, 1848–1888*, ed. George W. E. Russell (New York: Macmillan, 1895), 1:72.

10. Ibid., 69.

11. Arnold, "The Function of Criticism at the Present Time," p. 261.

12. Ibid., p. 271.

13. Critics debate whether Arnold resolves the tension between historical and ahistorical constructs in his work. Raymond Williams, with whom I agree, argues that Arnold reifies his notion of culture by treating it as an absolute while defining it as a process. *Culture and Society* (New York: Harper and Row, 1966), pp. 125–28. In "The Formal Nature of Victorian Thinking," Gerald Bruns argues that Arnold successfully resolves this contradiction. Culture, defined as a process regulated by an ideal, accommodates a belief in man's inherent perfectibility with the contingency of his existence as a historical being (p. 911).

In *The Victorian Critic and the Idea of History,* Peter Dale gives a detailed analysis of Arnold's accommodation of history with absolute value along lines similar to Bruns's argument. According to Dale, Arnold gets beyond the flux of history through an ideal of the best self, resting in the psychological and emotional constitution of human nature, ontologically independent of history, but realized only through historical process (pp. 118–29). Although I agree with both Bruns and Dale that Arnold indeed uses an ideal of human perfectibility that operates through history, I do not think his accommodation of that ideal to his sense of historical process is nearly as comfortable as Bruns and Dale suggest.

14. Arnold, *Culture and Anarchy,* ed. R. H. Super (Ann Arbor: University of Michigan Press, 1965), p. 94.

15. Arnold, *English Literature and Irish Politics,* pp. 163, 165.

16. Eliot, "Arnold and Pater," *Selected Essays,* pp. 382–93.

17. Pound, "Date Line," *Literary Essays,* p. 86.

18. See the debate in nos. 15, 16, and 17 of the *Victorian Newsletter:* Paul A. Cundiff, "Robert Browning: 'Our Human Speech,'" no. 15 (1959):1–9; Donald Smalley, "Browning's View of Fact in *The Ring and the Book,*" no. 16 (1959):1–9; Paul A. Cundiff, "Robert Browning: 'Indisputably Fact,'" no. 17 (1960):7–11; Robert Langbaum, "The Importance of Fact in *The Ring and the Book,*" no. 17 (1960):11–17. See also Paul F. Matheisen, "The Existential Aesthetic of Browning's *The Ring and the Book,*" *Literary Monographs* 3 (1970):164–84; Paul A. Cundiff, *Browning's Ring Metaphor and Truth* (Metuchen, N.J.: Scarecrow Press, 1972); Myron Tuman, "Browning's Historical Intention in *The Ring and the Book,*" *Studies in Browning and His Circle* 3 (1975):76–95.

19. Thomas Carlyle, "Boswell's Life of Johnson," *Critical and Miscellaneous Essays,* III, *Works,* 28:81.

20. Morse Peckham, "Browning's Historiography and *The Ring and the Book,*" *Victorian Poetry* 6 (1968):243–57. Roger Sharrock, "Browning and History," in *Robert Browning,* ed. Isobel Armstrong (Athens, Ohio: Ohio University Press, 1975), pp. 77–103.

21. R. G. Collingwood, *The Idea of History* (London: Oxford University Press, 1956), p. 199.

22. Ibid., p. 248.

23. In "Browning's Historiography and *The Ring and the Book,*" Morse Peckham argues that Browning builds into *The Ring and the Book* a confession of his own biases. I disagree, as my subsequent argument shows.

24. Langbaum, *The Poetry of Experience,* pp. 96–97.

25. See Henry Kozicki, *Tennyson and Clio: History in the Major Poems* (Baltimore: Johns Hopkins University Press, 1979), for an analysis of Tennyson's philosophy

of history. Kozicki argues that Tennyson reconciles the contradictions in his vision of history.

26. In "'The Lesser Faith': Hope and Reversal in *In Memoriam*," *Journal of English and Germanic Philology* 77 (1978):274–64, Gerald L. Bruns also argues that the form of *In Memoriam* allows Tennyson to pursue a dialectical mediation between contradictions.

27. Eliot, "In Memoriam," *Selected Essays*, p. 289.

28. Ibid., p. 291.

29. Culler, *The Poetry of Tennyson*, pp. 221–41.

30. T. S. Eliot, "The Method of Mr. Pound," *Athenaeum*, 24 October 1919, p. 1065.

31. Pound, *Letters*, p. 294; "How to Read," *Literary Essays*, p. 33.

32. Pound, *Gaudier-Brzeska*, p. 86.

33. Pound, *The ABC of Reading* (New York: New Directions, [1951]), p. 191; "Chinese Poetry—II," *Today* 3, no. 15 (May 1918):93.

34. Ronald Bush's study, *The Genesis of Ezra Pound's Cantos* (Princeton: Princeton University Press, 1976), contains an excellent discussion of the relationship of the Ur-Cantos to *Sordello* (pp. 75–86). Bush argues that Pound saw in *Sordello* the model of a new kind of narrative poetry that uses a paratactic overlayering of elements to portray the way in which a past history acquires significance to an individual intelligence. Bush feels that Pound originally conceived the poem as a "reticent autobiography," in which he adapted Jamesian techniques to poetry. According to Bush, Pound's later pronouncements about "ideogramic method" have caused critics to place a misleading emphasis upon the poem's ideogramic objectivity. Yet the tension between personal sensibility and imagistic objectivity is one characteristic of Pound from the beginning. It draws him to Browning and generates what seem to be contradictory constructional techniques for the poem.

35. Ezra Pound, *Lustra with Earlier Poems* (New York: Alfred A. Knopf, 1917), pp. 184–85.

36. Ibid., pp. 186–87.

37. Ibid., p. 182.

38. Michael Bernstein reads the metaphor in this way in *The Tale of the Tribe: Ezra Pound and the Modern Verse Epic* (Princeton: Princeton University Press, 1980), p. 166. Bernstein's very fine treatment of Pound's way of treating history at many points parallels my own.

39. Ezra Pound, *Selected Prose: 1909–1965*, ed. William Cookson (New York: New Directions, 1973), pp. 21–23. See also the discussions of this passage in Hugh Witemeyer, *The Poetry of Ezra Pound: Forms and Renewal, 1908–1920* (Berkeley: University of California Press, 1969), pp. 5–6; and Schneidau, *Ezra Pound: The Image and the Real*, pp. 65–68 and 116–18.

40. Those critics who address the problem of time in Ezra Pound's poetry emphasize his attempt to free man from time. In *The Barb of Time: On the Unity of Ezra Pound's Cantos* (New York: Oxford University Press, 1969), Daniel D. Pearlman argues that Pound's mind is fundamentally ahistorical, that he values events only as they imitate or repeat archetypes (pp. 24–28). I think that such an argument ignores the way in which the poem insists upon the material conditions of historical existence as a means of understanding spiritual activity. In *Time in Ezra Pound's Work* (Chapel Hill: University of North Carolina Press, 1977), William

Harmon also emphasizes Pound's attempt to transcend time, but he argues that *The Cantos* represent not the achieved product but the process of struggle involved in such an attempt.

41. Hugh Kenner, *The Poetry of Ezra Pound* (Norfolk, Conn.: New Directions, [1951]), p. 320.

42. T. S. Eliot, "*Ulysses*, Order, and Myth," *Dial* 75 (November 1923):483.

43. A. Walton Litz, "T. S. Eliot's Victorian Inheritance," *Nature and the Victorian Imagination*, ed. U. C. Knoepflmacher and G. B. Tennyson (Berkeley: University of California Press, 1977), pp. 482–88.

44. See James E. Miller, Jr., *T. S. Eliot's Personal Waste Land: Exorcism of the Demons* (University Park: University of Pennsylvania Press, 1977), pp. 1–6. In an NEH Seminar that I taught in 1980, Richard Lautz developed the parallels between the poems in great detail.

45. Eliot, "*In Memoriam*," pp. 391, 389.

46. In "The Myth and the Powerhouse," *The Myth and the Powerhouse* (New York: Farrar, Straus, and Giroux, 1965), pp. 3–21, Philip Rahv argues that the mythical method expresses a fear of history. Nonetheless, Rahv continues, Pound and Eliot still express the historicism of their age. I differ from Rahv in finding the conflict between myth and historicism in Pound and Eliot tenser and more deliberate than he finds it.

47. In *The Political Identities of Ezra Pound and T. S. Eliot* (Stanford: Stanford University Press, 1973), William M. Chace makes a similar point about Tiresias. He argues that the note about Tiresias "leads us to believe that the central 'personage' will be a so-called finite center resolving all experience by both undergoing it and describing it; in short, the consciousness of the poem. This would all be well, if we could be sure how to disentangle the consciousness that suffers from the one that observes. Such a distinction is as crucial as it is impossible. Although some readers of the poem would have us believe that consciousness is consciousness, as pudding is pudding, and that any consciousness is bound both to suffer and to observe, such a shaky assumption ignores the fact that suffering is of various kinds, the particular kinds largely determined by situations historical and otherwise, and that the purely objective consciousness, the Tiresias free of all partiality, is an imaginary entity put forward by those who wish to believe that partiality, characteristic of absolutely everyone, can be transcended" (p. 121).

48. Frederick Nietzsche, "The Use and Abuse of History," *The Complete Works of Frederick Nietzsche*, ed. Oscar Levy (New York: Russell and Russell, 1964), pp. 75, 12.

49. See Philip Fisher, "The Future's Past," *New Literary History* 6 (1975): 600–603.

50. Eliot, *Selected Essays*, p. 5.

51. Eliot, "Arnold and Pater," *Selected Essays*, p. 387.

52. T. S. Eliot, *Notes towards the Definition of Culture* (New York: Harcourt, Brace, 1949), p. 25.

53. Ibid., pp. 17–18.

54. Ibid., p. 86.

55. W. B. Yeats, *A Vision* (New York: Macmillan, 1956), p. 25.

56. Thomas Whitaker, *Swan and Shadow: Yeats's Dialogue with History* (Chapel Hill: University of North Carolina Press, 1964), p. 9.

57. Quoted in ibid., p. 245.

58. Yeats, "William Blake and the Imagination," *Essays and Introductions,* p. 114.

Chapter 5

1. Yeats, Introduction, *The Oxford Book of Modern Verse,* p. ix.
2. Yeats, *Essays and Introductions,* p. 494.
3. Pound, "The Prose Tradition in Verse," *Literary Essays,* p. 371.
4. Pound, "A Retrospect," *Literary Essays,* p. 11.
5. Eliot, "The Metaphysical Poets," *Selected Essays,* pp. 246, 247, 248.
6. Eliot, "Swinburne as Poet," *Selected Essays,* p. 285.
7. See particularly William E. Baker, *Syntax in English Poetry from Wyatt to Auden* (Berkeley: University of California Press, 1946), and Josephine Miles, *The Continuity of Poetic Language; The Primary Language of Poetry, 1540's–1940's* (New York: Octagon Books, 1965).
8. See particularly Hugh Kenner's *The Invisible Poet: T. S. Eliot* (New York: McDowell, Obolensky, 1959), and Thomas H. Jackson, *The Early Poetry of Ezra Pound,* for accounts of how Eliot and Pound used the resources of nineteenth-century rhetoric.
9. Eliot, "The Metaphysical Poets," *Selected Essays,* p. 246.
10. Pound, "A Retrospect," *Literary Essays,* p. 11.
11. Yeats, "Modern Poetry," *Essays and Introductions,* p. 497.
12. Pound, "A Retrospect," *Literary Essays,* p. 11.
13. George Eliot, *Middlemarch* (Boston: Houghton Mifflin, 1956), p. 23 (I:3).
14. See Boyd Litzinger and Donald Smalley, *Browning: The Critical Heritage* (London: Routledge and Kegan Paul, 1970), and Isobel Armstrong, *Victorian Scrutinies: Reviews of Poetry, 1830–1870,* pp. 50–59.
15. See *Tennyson: The Critical Heritage,* ed. John D. Jump (London: Routledge and Kegan Paul, 1967).
16. Eliot, *Selected Essays,* p. 248.
17. Pound associates such a reader with the opinion that "the Reverend Eliot has found a more natural language." Pound's statement suggests both his continued commitment to the difficulty of his method and Eliot's attempt, after his conversion, to change the way in which his writing addresses his audience.
18. Eliot, Preface to Perse, *Anabase,* p. 8.
19. In *T. S. Eliot and the Romantic Critical Tradition,* Edward Lobb makes an excellent analysis of the Romantic roots of Eliot's historiography (pp. 11–92).
20. "Coleridge," *Appreciations, with an essay on style* (London: Macmillan, 1915), pp. 65–104.
21. For a similar connection between Romantic and Modernist conceptions of reading, see Jane P. Tompkins, "The Reader in History," in *Reader Response: Criticism from Formalism to Post-Structuralism,* ed. Jane P. Tompkins (Baltimore: Johns Hopkins University Press, 1980), pp. 214–26.
22. In "Last Romantic or Last Victorian: Yeats, Tennyson, and Browning," George Bornstein makes a similar point in analyzing Yeats's relationship to Hallam and Tennyson (pp. 118–21).
23. *The Poems of Tennyson,* ed. Christopher Ricks, p. 400.
24. Eliot, "Arnold and Pater," *Selected Essays,* p. 392. For an account of the impressive coincidences between Eliot's work and Pater's, see William Blissett, "Pater and Eliot," *University of Toronto Quarterly* 22 (1953):261–68.

25. Walter Jackson Bate, *The Burden of the Past and the English Poet* (Cambridge: Belknap Press, 1970), p. 4.

26. Yeats, "A General Introduction for My Work," *Essays and Introductions,* p. 522.

27. Eliot, *Selected Essays,* p. 5.

28. Ibid., p. 13.

29. Thomas McFarland, "The Originality Paradox," *New Literary History* 5 (1974):447–76.

30. Pound, "How to Read," *Literary Essays,* p. 27.

31. Ibid., pp. 33–34.

32. Yeats, "Art and Ideas," *Essays and Introductions,* p. 355.

33. Eliot, "Arnold and Pater," *Selected Essays,* p. 393.

34. Harold Bloom, *The Anxiety of Influence* (Oxford: Oxford University Press, 1973), p. 30.

35. Yeats, *Autobiography,* p. 93.

36. *The Letters of W. B. Yeats,* ed. Allan Wade (New York: Macmillan, 1959), p. 759. See also Bloom, *Yeats,* pp. 331–32.

37. See Ian Gregor, "Eliot and Matthew Arnold," in *Eliot in Perspective: A Symposium,* ed. Graham Martin (New York, 1970), pp. 267–78, for an excellent account of the relationship.

38. Eliot, "Arnold and Pater," *Selected Essays,* p. 392.

39. Pound, "Lionel Johnson," *Literary Essays,* p. 362, and "Translators of Greek: Early Translators of Homer," *Literary Essays,* p. 270.

40. Pound, *Literary Essays,* p. 227.

41. Edmund Clarence Stedman, *Victorian Poets,* (Boston: James R. Osgood, 1876), p. 413.

42. Paul de Man, "Literary History and Literary Modernity," *Blindness and Insight: Essays in the Rhetoric of Contemporary Criticism* (New York: Oxford University Press, 1971), pp. 142–65.

43. T. S. Eliot, "To Criticize the Critic," *To Criticize the Critic and Other Writings* (London: Faber and Faber, 1965), p. 16.

44. Claudio Guillen, *Literature as System: Essays toward the Theory of Literary History* (Princeton: Princeton University Press, 1971), pp. 432–33.

45. Ibid., pp. 425–27.

Index

Index